Seeds
in the Wind

RICK WIENECKE

Unless otherwise noted, all Scripture quotations are taken from the King James Bible. The KJV is public domain in the United States.

ISBN 978-965-7542-34-7

Photo Credits:
Geoff Barnard, Petra van der Zande, Rick Wienecke

Cover art by Kevin Moffatt - MannaArt.com. Used with permission.

Order information:

Website: http://www.castingseeds.com
Email: castingseeds@gmail.com

Editing and Lay-out:
Petra van der Zande, Tsur Tsina Publications, Jerusalem, Israel.

Printed in Israel by PRINTIV, Jerusalem

Dedication

Wholeheartedly I want to dedicate this book

to an amazing God. In His kindness He has given

me a Savior a Lord and a friend in Jesus.

He has given me Dafna, Daniel and Yohai -

a wonderful wife and two great sons.

He shares His love and tears with me

over His people and His land.

I want to thank and bless all of our friends who

have had a part in making this book happen.

You know who you are, but more important:

God knows who you are.

Table of Contents

Chapter 1   "This is our home! Not a museum!"   7

Chapter 2   Cross Country Canada   11

Chapter 3   A Starry Night in an Open Field   15

Chapter 4   Discovering *Exodus*   19

Chapter 5   Entebbe Rescue   23

Chapter 6   Preparing for the Israeli Kibbutz Experience   27

Chapter 7   Saying Good-bye   35

Chapter 8   The Last Christmas at Home   39

Chapter 9   Airport Drama   41

Chapter 10   Welcome to Israel!   45

Chapter 11   Lost and Found in Haifa   49

Chapter 12   Meeting Arthur Blessitt   55

Chapter 13   Kibbutz Life   57

Chapter 14   Isaiah 14   63

Chapter 15   Miracle at *Misrad haPnim*   67

Chapter 16   Dafna's Story   71

Chapter 17   First Encounter with Rick   73

Chapter 18   "You are my best friend ever...."   75

Chapter 19   "...And I will go anywhere with you!"   79

Chapter 20   Wedding, Honeymoon, Life on the Kibbutz   81

Chapter 21   Spreading our Wings   83

Chapter 22   Visiting the Grandparents in Toronto   85

Chapter 23   From Lake Cottage to Colorado Mountain Cabin   87

Chapter 24   Learning to Trust and Obey   91

Chapter 25   The Foundry apprentice   95

Chapter 26   Return to the Colorado Mountains   97

Chapter 27   Intercession in Samaria   103

Chapter 28   The Haifa Conference   111

Table of Contents

Chapter 29	The 'Payback' Word	115
Chapter 30	The Seven Last Words	121
Chapter 31	A Heavenly Commission	127
Chapter 32	Sculpting and Meditating	131
Chapter 33	Encounter with the Model for the Holocaust	133
Chapter 34	Redeployment and a Voice Crying in the Wilderness	139
Chapter 35	Gethsemane	145
Chapter 36	Two Evil Designs for a Violent Death	149
Chapter 37	The Face of a Sad Angel	153
Chapter 38	"Father, forgive them!"	157
Chapter 39	"Today, you will be with me in paradise!!	161
Chapter 40	"Mother, see your son. Son, here is your mother."	163
Chapter 41	"My God, my God! Why have You forsaken me?"	167
Chapter 42	"I thirst!"	173
Chapter 43	"It is finished!"	175
Chapter 44	"Into Your hands...."	177
Chapter 45	Butterfly	179
Chapter 46	Final Embrace	185
Chapter 47	A "Fountain of Tears" in Arad	187
Chapter 48	A "Fountain of Tears" in Birkenau - the Journey	191
Chapter 49	The Return of the "Lion of Judah"	207
Chapter 50	Appendix	215

Visitors looking at the exposition in the backyard

CHAPTER 1

"This is our home! Not a museum!"

"Dad, what are you trying to do? This is crazy! This is a home, our home! Not a museum!"
Yohai, our teenage son, sounded really angry this time. He had woken up late after being out all night with his friends. Getting out of bed, wearing only his boxers, he had stumbled into four elderly German ladies who were waiting in line to use our downstairs bathroom.

"I am out of here!" Yohai fumed. "Dad! You're putting a sixty foot wall with seven crucifixion scenes and seven bronze figures representing the Holocaust in our backyard! Dougi [1] and I have been thinking about getting an apartment in Tel Aviv, and if I even see just one 'Black Hat' [ultra-Orthodox Jew] in front of our home, I'm leaving. I'm gone!" he threatened. "What were you on [2] when you thought of this?"

The day had begun normally, and during the morning hours I had been working on a commission for a bronze sculpture in my studio. Even though "The Fountain of Tears" wasn't completed yet, we had been receiving small groups to view the sculptured Fountain of Tears exhibit in the large courtyard behind our home. The German group of about 35 people who arrived at 3 p.m. had been the reason for Yohai's outburst. My son and I were now alone in my studio, just staring at each other. Yohai's eyes were wide with rage while he waited for my response. What could I say to him? How did this all begin?

In 2005, after moving to Arad I proceeded with the assembly of the 'Fountain' in our backyard. People began to talk about this project in small circles, then they began phoning to ask if they could see the artwork.

---

[1] Dougi was Yohai's friend.
[2] "What were you on?" is a drugs related expression, meaning, "Are you stoned? Hallucinating?"

My family was in the process of learning how to live with a large piece of artwork that gradually was becoming more known - a fact that every artist would welcome. However, all the commissioned, life-sized sculptures I had made over the years eventually had left the workshop, giving me a sense of completion. But the "Fountain", my largest piece of art and one I struggled for a long time to make, didn't leave home but stayed in our back yard. What was more, from a Jewish viewpoint, it had been Christianity historically condemning the Jews for Jesus' crucifixion, that created the foundations for the Holocaust. *How could I create something that reflected the relationship between the Holocaust and the crucifixion?* I wondered. *This is crazy! Yohai is probably right. What was I thinking?*

By exclaiming, "This is Israel! Don't you know where you live?" Yohai meant something more than a geographic entity. He was right, Israel is more than a concept - it is also a nation.

> ***Oh that my head were waters,***
> ***and mine eyes a fountain of tears,***
> ***that I might weep day and night***
> ***for the slain of the daughter of my people!***
> Jeremiah 9:1 KJV

These words had been a part of the initiating of The Fountain of Tears. **My** people. My **people**. Those words touched me so deeply. So much history has been attached to Jeremiah's tears. The ones I shed became markers, milestones along a journey that led me, the "Gentile", to be attached to this people, Israel. Could I dare to say, or perhaps whisper, **"My people"**?

So what Yohai meant was, "Don't you realize where you live? This is Israel! What you have in our backyard is very controversial." He was concerned that the ultra-Orthodox, religious Jews would stage a mass protest in front of our house.

"I completely understand and totally agree with you," I told my son. "You have no idea how much. But Yohai, I had to create this. I just had to."

The fact that I understood his frustration didn't solve the problem, but at least we had been able to speak about it.

"If you feel you have to leave home," I told him, "you'll probably learn a lot from the experience. I want you to know that you can always come back home. But," I warned him, "I cannot undo what I have done with the 'Fountain'."

When he turned to leave the studio, I realized he was almost the same age I had been when I had left home. Even though he was younger in age, he was much more mature than I had been back then. During their three year army service Israeli teens mature so quickly.
The moment he entered the IDF (Israel Defense Force) my son would become an adult.

Alone in my studio I tried to reflect on our heated discussion.
The 'Fountain' had triggered quite a few dilemmas in the past and I knew there would be more in the future. Would one of them cause him to pack up his belongings and move out? Tears stung my eyes. Was all this worth it? For what? Did I really understand what I was doing with this work, the 'Fountain of Tears'? What is this stirring inside of me? Am I artistically inspired? What does it actually mean: reflection in suffering, a fellowship? Throughout history, haven't these two personalities of the Holocaust and the Crucifixion of Jesus always opposed each other? Who was I to try and connect the two?
"My people", I thought again. *Why do I feel so attached to them? And this land, Israel, where many have been surprised to hear that I have Israeli Citizenship."*

My thoughts drifted back to how it had all started, to the time I left my parent's home in Ontario, Canada. At the age of nineteen, I was on my way to Vancouver in search of new and untold adventures.

CHAPTER 2

Cross Country Canada

Ten days of driving across Canada was amazing, despite the constant tension caused by wondering if my old (1965) Volkswagen van would make it to the end of the day. I drank in the huge skies of the Canadian Prairie provinces along with the never ending sunsets; it was like going through wide pallets of colors. To help enhance the many miles and long hours of driving, I smoked and shared hash with my two American hitchhikers.

Even though during high school hash and marijuana always had been part of my weekends, I somehow had managed to stay away from the heavier drugs, although I never figured out why. Instinctively I had drawn a line that I wasn't willing to cross. Soft drugs put me into a happy state of mind, uncontrollable fits of laughter and silliness. I enjoyed those, but once in a while I lost control. When that happened, a deep fear came over me, a foreboding, and the resulting panic made me want to disappear but never enough to quit the drugs.

Arriving in Vancouver gave me a feeling of accomplishment, but soon the newness of the West Coast became the routine of my former lifestyle. My life's motto was to enjoy myself. It was very important to me. The reason I had a job was to earn enough money to be able to do just that. Because self-pleasure governed my life there was nothing that could stop me; I never thought about the consequences this motto could have for me or for others.

Girls and drinking were for pleasure and by sticking to the rules of the "hunt" at the bars and discos I had my share of successes.

I met a girl in a bar one night and, after a short period of time, we agreed to live together. One evening we had been drinking a lot of beer when she suddenly asked, "Do you think there is a God?"
I didn't like that question which forced me to think about something other than myself. I told her that I dismissed the Big Bang Theory. I didn't believe that a big explosion, billions of years ago, put our universe into order. "I believe there has to be a creator," I told her. "The array of colors in the fall when the leaves change has to be an intentional creative act, not just random chance."
The answer surprised me and seemed to satisfy her and the moment of thinking about something other than ourselves passed as quickly as it arrived. *Yes, it is good to know there is a God*, I thought, *but who cares?* Returning to the things that were really important, we ordered another round of beer.

After a few months, our relationship began to cool; the spontaneity was no longer there; we had begun to know each other too well.
It was time for me to move on.

In an old Victorian home in downtown Vancouver, I rented a cheap basement apartment which had a cavernous feel. In order to earn my keep I became a taxi cab driver.
One rainy Sunday evening, things were slow, and most of the drivers were parked in different parts of the city waiting for their turn. Being the next cab on call, I waited in my car that was parked in the lot next to the dispatching office. Suddenly the passenger door opened and Antonio jumped in, a big smile on his face. The Portuguese guy was usually happy, but this time there was something special going on.
     "Guess what I got?" He didn't wait for me to guess. "Columbian! Laced with acid."
I wasn't exactly sure what that meant. I knew that Columbian marijuana was some of the best, a more potent "high" than most. *But how can you mix it with acid?* I wondered.
As it was a slow night anyway, I decided it didn't matter and we were going to smoke the joint.
Just as Antonio and I finished smoking, the dispatch radio came to life telling me to pick up somebody from a rural town about fifteen

minutes away. I hoped that by the time I had reached the address the smell of the drugs would have left the car, but because of the heavy rain I couldn't keep the window open.

The effect of the marijuana hit me about ten minutes into the drive – much quicker than usual and far more aggressively. Suddenly, it felt as if something came down on me and I was gripped by fear. My heart rate went up, and by the time I entered the small town, paranoia had taken over.

Even though I knew the area, I had trouble finding the street number, and I was struggling to keep calm as the pounding raindrops on the car window drove me crazy. In the end the address turned out to be a little church. I pulled up in front and kept the motor running, while my head and thoughts were racing and my heart pounding. *If I can just hold on to the steering wheel I'll be okay*, I thought.

The church was a typical white building, with a tall, sharp roof and a cross on its highest point.

Staring at the two large front doors of the church, I kept hoping that whoever the customers were, they wouldn't come out.

A moment later the doors opened and a group of old ladies walked towards my cab. They all looked the same, with short white hair, and like the water streaming down the car windows, they flowed towards the car.

A voice in my head kept saying, "Don't open the doors! Don't let them come in!" However, the car doors opened and one by one they entered the taxi. Two ladies slid beside me while three others filled the back seat to capacity.

I came very close to losing it. Without looking at any of them I drove away slowly, struggling to keep the car on the road. Thankfully, it was only a short trip to the nursing home where they lived.

After receiving my fare, I quickly drove away. A few hundred feet further down the road I pulled the car over and shut off the engine.

All I could do was sit there and breathe deeply. I was so afraid, so terribly afraid. Bad things sometimes happened to me when I was stoned, but I never had had such a horrific experience.

CHAPTER 3

A Starry Night in an Open Field

Memories of that evening stayed with me for a long time. I didn't know what to do, or if I was supposed to do anything. I always had been able to brush things off, refocus, carry on, and look for the next adventure. This time I couldn't. For the first time in my life I felt desperate and alone.

A few evenings later I took my dog for a walk and sat down on the grass of a quiet field far away from everything.. The clear night sky was filled with millions of stars. The beauty and vastness of the universe pulled me out of myself and consumed me for that one still moment. I was surprised when the silence was broken by my own voice, "If there is anyone up there, I want to give up all this junk." It was a kind of prayer. Reflecting upon my life, I felt inwardly dirty, a filth that had been accumulating but which couldn't be washed away or ignored any longer. There even seemed to be a smell attached to it – it reeked of death.
For days I thought about the short conversation that night in the field. Debating with myself that it was nonsense, I desperately hoped no one had seen me. If by any chance people had overheard me, they would have presumed I was talking to the dog. Making an effort to convince myself to get over it, I tried to return to the life I had always known. However, that smell continued to linger.
In the end I decided to do something, to respond somehow to what I had said: the junk had to be dealt with and so I thought maybe I could quit smoking cigarettes. According to the warning on each package, cigarettes were bad for your health, so this seemed like a reasonable decision. It was reasonable, for about the first four hours, but then
I realized how much I liked smoking, how I craved the nicotine.

Cigarettes created a certain order in my day. I ate certain foods because a cigarette tasted better afterwards.

Drinking beer without smoking was unthinkable. I was not planning to give up beer, but how could I drink without my cigarettes?

Suddenly, my whole life was in turmoil.

After struggling to live three days without cigarettes, I felt like I was going to die. I realized that cigarettes had been such a big part of my life, and so my response to the moment of drama in the field began to be less and less important.

That night my taxi rides were irritating - mostly short distances and no tips. The weather was cold and it looked like there was going to be snow, or maybe just a cold freezing rain. Most of the clients were drunks trying to get home by riding in a cab instead of endangering their lives by walking. I was lucky to get one dollar and fifty cents for a ride, let alone a tip. It wasn't only irritation from work, but also the third day without a cigarette. *Why am I doing this?* I asked myself. *Not smoking is really stupid!*

The moment I declared my stupidity, the front passenger door was jerked open. A hand grabbed the front seat, and then a man's head, another arm, and a pair of legs entered, seemingly independent of each other. The struggling body parts came together with a stream of swear words coming out of a mouth. While trying to get into a sitting position, the man cursed each and everything. Hunched over in the car seat, he tried to catch his breath, turned to me and tried to tell me his address. It took three efforts until I made out enough legible words to understand where he wanted to go. Immediately, the car was filled with his drunken stench. It was the worst of all smells, because he wasn't just someone who drank too much; in his case, the alcohol had consumed him. This man had not been drinking for one evening, but he looked like he had been going on for days. I was amazed he could even remember his address.

Having a general idea where the house was, I was sure it would be an empty one - nobody could live with such a man. How he had made it across the street from the hotel bar to the taxi stand defied all logic.

For about ten minutes the man sat quietly in his seat, and I thought he had fallen asleep. Suddenly he stirred and began to mumble to himself; then he became agitated and rummaged through his pockets. He relaxed when he found what he had been looking for. Leaning against the car seat, he took a cigarette out of a beat-up box. Managing to coordinate the lighter with the end of the cigarette, he lit up and inhaled.

Until that very moment everything about this passenger had looked and smelled pretty bleak. All of a sudden, a lightness entered my soul and I had a sense of reprieve, even rescue.

This broken and miserable human being was going to save me. *I'm not really smoking*, I thought, *I will only inhale what he blows out.* It was a strange switch, because my previous disgust turned into one of appreciation and even a feeling of friendship.

Due to the early winter, the night was so cold that we had to keep the car windows closed, preventing the smoke from escaping. As I waited for the cigarette smoke to reach me, I felt happy for the first time in days. When it whirled around my face, I deeply inhaled it, but to my surprise, instead of enjoying the effect, everything in me revolted, recoiled. It is hard to describe the sense of shock that I felt.

The smoke had become vile, foreign to me, something I had never known. My old "friend" had made me sick, causing my stomach to revolt to such an extent that I was going to throw up. Quickly cranking down the car window, I no longer cared about the cold because I desperately needed some fresh air.

With my head partially out of the window, not only did I deeply inhale the fresh air, but I also tried to separate myself physically from the smoke.

My passenger couldn't figure out why it suddenly had become so cold and windy inside the taxi. When he realized that I had rolled down the window and that I wasn't about to close it again, he deluged me with every nasty word he was able to remember. I didn't care. The fact he refused to pay me for the ride didn't bother me either.

On my way back to town I tried to understand what had just happened. No longer did I understand who I was; inside something had
changed. Something that once had been very important to me had
been taken from me. It was as if I had never smoked in my life and
I knew I would never smoke again.

But there was more. Pulling the car to the side of the road I just sat
there. Staring straight ahead, I didn't want to think but couldn't help
myself. *Somebody changed me, but I had nothing to do with that
change*, I thought. Suddenly I became afraid. *Who changed me? Who
did this? Did He hear me in the field? What am I really thinking?
And who is He? I have to find out, I have to!*

Thus began my search for God - this "He". I knew that this was outside
of my realm, something beyond what I could see, and something
outside my natural senses. He was something or someone spiritual,
whatever that meant.

CHAPTER 4

Discovering *Exodus*

While hunting for the truth, I tried different forms of meditation, mind expansion and all kinds of diets.
Even though I wanted to find 'Him', if He was really there, I wanted Him to show Himself to me. In my heart I knew He existed, but I didn't dare say this out loud. The thought scared and attracted me at the same time.

One slow day I was in my basement apartment, feeling utterly bored. It was one of those days I couldn't find anything to do or make something happen. Even the air seemed heavy and used, which didn't come as a surprise because everything in that basement was old and discarded. Most of the furniture had been kept because of some kind of delusional thought of future use.

I stayed in my small bedroom with my only true friend, a sixteen inch TV for company, cutting myself off from the trash on the other side of the door. That other side was a world full of musty things in cardboard boxes that even memory had left behind and of crooked metal shelves that never stood straight, filled with old books in all kinds of shapes and sizes. Soon, within the next half hour, maybe my boredom would end with a TV program. Returning from the bathroom, I glanced at some of the books on the shelf and even touched them lightly with my finger - something that I had never done before.
Reading was something I always avoided, and I could never understand why people made such a fuss over it. My parents both loved to read, and my older sister also was a bookworm. They would always say something like, "This is so good, I can't put it down!" or, "Let me know when you have finished it." The hardest one for me to believe was, "The movie was good, but the book is so much better."

Whatever happens, I thought, *I am not going to fight my boredom by reading a book.*

I always used to brag about the fact that I had finished high school without hardly reading a book, an attitude which had been held in high esteem by my friends. But they were a long way from me right now, and I had to wait another fifteen minutes before the four o'clock program. Picking a book up at random, I headed for my room while rubbing my dusty hands off on my pants.

The only chair in my room was old and comfortable. I didn't open the book right away, but I turned it over a few times in my hand. Somehow the title, *Exodus*, rang a tiny bell in my head, and I remembered a movie had been made of it. *Perhaps there are some pictures in it,* I thought. *How bad can it be? Only ten more minutes to kill before the TV program. Anything will be better than reading this book.*

The few black and white pictures inside the book didn't mean anything to me. However, the moment I began to read I was pulled into the story. It began quickly with a mix of things. A reporter meeting an old friend, a nurse on vacation in Cypress, this caught my interest.

Then there was an old ship full of children, Jewish children. Even though there were many things I didn't understand, for some reason I didn't want to stop. *I'll read until four thirty,* I decided.

Gradually, the story became more complicated as more names were introduced like Haganah, Palestine, the British Mandate, and Holocaust. There was much more I didn't understand but by then I had forgotten the time. When it became too dark for me to read, I pushed the chair closer to the only light in the room. Eventually I fell asleep in the chair with the book on my lap.

The next morning, I wanted to continue reading but had to go to work. That day, I did everything I had to do and quickly returned home to continue reading. This pattern continued throughout the week, and even during work my thoughts kept drifting back to the story.

It seemed my apartment had come alive, as if someone was waiting for me, expecting me. It was exciting.

The moment I sat in my chair I was pulled back into the world of *Exodus.* It was a place of struggle, not only against the Germans, but also the British, Russians or Poles.

For these Jews it was a struggle against a two-thousand-year separation from a land that now seemed ready to open her doors to her ancient people after the biggest devastation in their history - the Holocaust. **Holocaust** was a word that seemed to stand alone against the backdrop of all the other names that I was being introduced to within this book. It was the word that threaded together the complex viewpoints of each of the people groups represented within the story. *Why does this story seem to possess my life?* I wondered. *Not only am I actually reading a book, but I'm learning about a history connected to a people that is so foreign, so far away from me.* I kept on reading.

Through the personalities in the story, Leon Uris explained history by telling about the Jewish suffering in the Russian Empire at the end of the 1800's. I read about young Jews emigrating to Ottoman Palestine to form communal farms. The Jews left Europe because they were being persecuted, but at the same time they were inwardly, spiritually drawn back to this Israel.

I learned about the concentration camps, the cattle cars, the death camps, the death marches, the piles of corpses not yet burned in the ovens. Also about those other bodies which, until this very day, have not been discovered in the dark places of distant forests. The information shocked me deeply and was almost impossible to comprehend. This part of the book seemed to stop me, because I had known nothing about the Holocaust. My main source of information, the TV, had taught me through enumerable movies about WW2 that the Americans were always the good guys and the Germans the bad guys.

My knowledge of the Middle East was equally pitiful. International news didn't interest me at all. To me, the Middle East was always a war waiting to happen. As long as it didn't affect my Friday or Saturday night, it wasn't important; so I didn't care.
By reading this book, something within me had changed. *Should I stop now, after reading half of the book?* I wondered. *Do I need to know more? Perhaps I should go back to being normal.*
Yet, I couldn't help myself, and kept reading.

When I reached the period of the War of Independence, the book gave detailed information which boiled down to the fact that the Jews were massively outnumbered and didn't have enough arms. Three of the seven Arab armies attacking Israel had been trained by the British and were well equipped. I suddenly realized that for the Jews this war could have easily been the last step to the "Final Solution" that Hitler had had in mind. When I read about the War of Independence that birthed the State of Israel in 1948, I felt myself becoming more and more emotionally attached. *They couldn't have won,* I thought, *but they did.* A group of people, that only three years before had lost two-thirds of their population in Europe. They had waged an impossible war. Their survival had been a miracle.

Suddenly a thought hit me, *If there is a God up there, and I am beginning to think there is, He must have something to do with these Jews. I have to find out what they are into.*

CHAPTER 5

Entebbe Rescue

After finishing the book I read it a second time and began to check out some of the historical facts that were mentioned. The majority of them I found to be accurate. Then I began to look for books about the Holocaust and the beginning of Israel as a state. I read them all hungrily. I was moving towards something, what I didn't know, but I felt that something was pulling me. I knew that it had something to do with Him.

On June 27, 1976, while driving into Vancouver, I absentmindedly played with the radio in search of some music. Usually, when hitting a news station, I quickly moved the dial. However, when I heard the word "Israel" I adjusted the knob to get a clearer reception.
The deep, serious voice of the announcer reported about the hijacking of Air France flight 139 en-route from Tel Aviv to Paris. The plane had

been taken over by German terrorists connected to the Palestinian Liberation Organization. On board were foreign Jews, Israelis and people of other nationalities. The hostages were taken to Entebbe Airport in Uganda, Africa, and upon arrival the Jews were separated from the others.

Something jarred me. Feeling emotionally connected, I was eager to know what the government of Israel was going to do.
The hijackers demanded the release of a large number of PLO fighters from Israeli prisons in exchange for the lives of the Jews.
If the demands were not met, the hijackers would begin killing the hostages within a few hours.

Entebbe Airport in Uganda

Why? I wondered. *Why are their lives so valuable!? Somehow Jews are always bartered, but more often they are sought out for killing.*

Throughout the following days this question kept nagging at me as I tried to keep abreast of news reports about the hijacking. The Jews were being held in a different room in the airport. Why were they separated from the other passengers? Was this another "selection"– a heavy-laden word to a Holocaust survivor - and now again it was being used by and implemented by Germans? I learned that during the first 24 hours an agreement had been reached to give Israel a few days to decide. At least they had some breathing space.

Days later, on July 4, while driving on the highway into Vancouver, I worked the radio dials to find a news station. Because the terrorists' deadline was looming, I was afraid of what I might hear. At the same time wondering why I was concerned, why I felt empathy, I kept turning the dials until I heard a voice. My heart skipped a beat when I heard shouting, laughing, and a lot of people talking at the same time. And there was singing!? With an emotion-filled voice, the broadcaster tried to describe the scene at the tarmac of Ben Gurion Airport in Tel Aviv.

He was surrounded by the rescued Jews who had come home safely from Entebbe. The reporter spoke about the IDF soldiers and the passengers that now were safe. All he got from one of the passengers was a sentence  choked by tears. They had been saved! I couldn't believe my ears!

By way of an incredibly complex and dangerous mission, Israel had sent an elite group of soldiers to rescue their own. This time, the selection had failed – the Jews lived!
It's impossible to describe what happened to me at that moment, but it was as if something went off in me; something erupted and was trying to find a way out. I pulled the car to the shoulder of the road and began to weep, then sob, while on the radio the cheering and shouting continued.

It was all so strange, so not me. *Why do I feel this for somebody I don't even know?* I wondered.
Suddenly everything became clear to me and I knew for certain:
I have to go and see that place, this Israel!

.

CHAPTER 6

Preparing for the Israeli Kibbutz Experience

Leaving Vancouver was more complicated than I had expected. If my destination was Israel, how was I going to manage this? The basic plan was to spend six months in Israel and then backpack through Europe. My guess was that this would take me a whole year.
Pondering the problem of how to support myself while in Israel, I figured there would be American or Canadian companies who needed English speakers and could possibly offer me a job.

In a letter to the Israeli Embassy in Ottawa, I wrote about my travel plans and asked if they had a list of foreign companies in Israel. Within two weeks they sent a reply, including a list of about twenty- five different companies in Israel that had their mother company in North America. The letter from the Israeli Embassy seemed to make my travel plans more feasible, and I was becoming more encouraged. Carefully I screened company names and contact information.
At the bottom of the page I noticed an address in Vancouver of a Jewish community center. *I didn't know that there was a Jewish center in Vancouver,* I thought. *But why would I be surprised? Until a few weeks ago I didn't even know there were Jews.*

The community center would be a good place to start as it was in a downtown area that I knew. While driving to the center that particular morning, I questioned my actions. Writing the letter to the embassy had come in a response to an emotional encounter that I didn't yet understand. The book *Exodus* had been a beginning, but it was just a book, a well-crafted story woven historically into a relationship with a country and a people. But in every other way Israel hadn't existed for me.

The dramatic piece of recent history from the Entebbe rescue had brought me closer to reality. I wondered what my visit to this center would bring.

The two-story building had a large Star of David over the main entrance. In the main foyer I glanced at the listed offices with their corresponding floors and room numbers until I presumably found the correct one - Israel Information Department, room thirty-seven, second floor. *I'm taking the stairs,* I thought. *The elevator is too fast. I need time to think. I'm about to come into contact with a real person.* This time, it wasn't a book or a news broadcast or a letter. No, this time it would be for real. I needed time to think about the questions I was going to ask the person I was going to see.

As I slowly climbed higher and higher, the more nervous I became, and by the time I reached room thirty-seven, my head seemed to swirl. Under the Israel Department sign was a large poster depicting a beautiful, fertile valley that looked like a neatly sown quilt of fields. Each square had a different crop in a different color, as if laid out in a crafted order. Across the background, like a wall guarding the valley, were large, rolling hills. "Hula" I read at the bottom of the poster. *Must be a place in Israel,* I thought. The valley seemed to swallow up all my questions and calm my nerves. The picture was so wonderful and welcoming.

However, the moment I entered the office, the feeling of tranquility left me. The small room had just enough space for a large, old, wooden desk with equally old, wooden chairs. Sitting down on one of them, I looked around, hoping it had been all right to walk in unannounced. Hardly an inch of wall space showed; pictures and notes were pinned everywhere. Some of them seemed official and important, while others looked like old shopping lists. The messy office had a relaxing effect on me. When things are too formal, I usually feel on edge. Somehow I knew that the fact I had not made an appointment wouldn't matter too much.

I had been waiting about ten minutes when the door behind the big desk suddenly opened. Her arms full of files and folders, a young woman bumped her way in.

As she dropped into her chair, the files landed safely on the desk, and she let out a long sigh of relief. And then she noticed me sitting there.

"Hi!" she said and I replied likewise. "I hope you haven't waited long." She pushed the files to one side. "I've been trying to get to these reports for two weeks".

They'll probably move from the desk to the walls in a few days, I thought while nodding and smiling.

"I'm Sarah Cohen," she introduced herself. "I'm the secretary to the *shaliach*, that's the Israeli representative who is in charge of help-ing people from the Jewish community in the area immigrate to Israel. We are a bridge between the Diaspora and The Land, Israel."

Sarah was warm and friendly. "I'm sorry that Motti, the *shaliach*, is not here today, but maybe I can help you. Do you have a question?"

I told her that I was interested in visiting Israel and wondered about staying there for six months. "The Israeli Embassy gave me a list with company names," I showed her the letter. "Can you recommend one of them?"

Completely disregarding my letter, Sarah said, "If you are going for six months, then why not work on a kibbutz? I worked on a kibbutz this last summer; you get a place to live, food, and a little pocket money". Without pausing for breath, she continued, "If you are there that long, they even offer an *ulpan*, that's where you learn Hebrew half the day and the other half you work. I think that runs for six months!"

"Would it matter that I'm not Jewish?" I asked.

When Sarah began to rummage through the papers on her desk, I wondered if she had not heard me until, with a big smile, she pulled a colored brochure from a large pile of papers. Continuing to ignore me she read through the leaflet and then said, "Nope, no problem. They allow ten percent non-Jews to attend *ulpan*, so you are in. Here, take a look."

Looking at the pictures, I saw men and woman dressed in T-shirts, shorts and sandals and more pictures of the wonderful, quilted fields. I didn't realize then just how well this office represented Israel: b*eauty in the midst of managed chaos.*

"You can keep the brochure," Sarah said smiling, "It's a miracle I found it."

At least, I thought, *it will be spared being pinned upside down on the wall.* I was happy to receive it.

Visiting the community center had been another big step forward. There seemed to be a growing momentum, like a river pushing me in a determined direction. Even though I didn't understand what was happening, I experienced a deep quiet inside of me. It was if someone was telling me, "It's okay. Just go with the flow."

But there were other reasons I wanted to leave Vancouver. A number of times, I borrowed money using my old Datsun station wagon as collateral without telling the bank managers about my other existing loans.

By now the bankers had begun to realize that this one car couldn't be divided into pieces when I didn't make my monthly payments.

I knew I was in trouble. And on top of that, there was this issue of my driver's license. I had so many tickets that the police wanted to revoke my license.

Knowing the notice would be in the mail soon, I had to leave British Columbia and be back in Ontario before the letter arrived. Once there, I could switch my old license for a new Ontario one.

Packing everything I owned, which wasn't much, I bought a one-way plane ticket back home. The last thing I did was to put my car keys in a little box which I mailed to one of the bank managers. I don't think the accompanying letter of apology consoled him much.

The idea of returning to Ontario triggered a lot of mixed feelings. On the one hand, it would be good to see my family and old friends; but I wondered, *What will they think of my plans of going to Israel and working on a kibbutz? What am I going to answer when they ask me "Why?"*

I knew most of my friends wouldn't understand if I honestly told them,

"Because I am looking for God and I think He has something to do with these Jews."

"God? The Holocaust? The beginning of Israel as a state?"

All these would come out in the form of questions, questions that I couldn't answer. How could I? I too had no answers, only questions. My family would think I was crazy, and rightly so.

I decided to make life easy for myself by simply not telling them. My plan was to live with my parents, get a job to earn money and then, when I had my tickets, passport and all the necessary forms filled out, only then would I let them know where I was going. And in case my parents freaked out, I surmised, it would be just a short time before I left.

Everything seemed to go according to plan: while staying with my parents, I worked in a huge warehouse and did as much overtime as I could in order to save money.

Sarah Cohen had given me the name of the *shaliach* in Toronto, with whom I met in secret. Finding some excuse to be in the city, Shaul and I met each other once every two weeks in the Toronto Jewish Community Center. There, they interviewed me, gave me forms to fill out, and I even had to pass a medical examination. Shaul was a friendly and helpful man who checked out everything. He advised me, showed me maps and gave me other information and even told me his own personal story.

After a few months of covert trips into Toronto, everything that needed to be done was finished: the papers were collected and all the necessary forms filled out and sent to the central office in the US and several different *kibbutzim*. The only thing I now had to do was wait until Shaul informed me which kibbutz accepted me and when.

By the end of November I had been working steadily for about three months. In order to save time and money, I had been riding a ten speed bicycle to work, but now winter was setting in and the riding became very cold.

All this time my parents had been great, and it was like we were becoming friends. We had long talks together, something that had never really happened before. I enjoyed those good months we spent together. I am sure they wanted to ask what was going on with me, but probably they were afraid our relationship would change if they drew too much attention to the change itself.

They were not used to seeing me so serious and focused. I didn't go out much with friends, was not getting drunk or stoned, not even on my weekends.

They realized I had less of a temper and swore less, and that I had somehow changed. I felt they treated me like a rare butterfly: the moment you come too close to take a good look it flies away, never to return. So my parents enjoyed the new Rick but kept their distance, until their curiosity could not be contained any longer.

On a particular Sunday I had planned to do an evening shift to get some more overtime, but it didn't work out. Instead, after dinner my parents and I went to the living room where we plopped in comfortable chairs. As none of us had to go out or do anything in particular, we began to talk in general about local politics, a possible strike at General Motors, or the weather. We wondered if it was going to be an early winter.

"I'm surprised you continue to ride your bike these frigid days," Dad said to me. "You better start thinking of buying a car for the winter."

For a bystander, this might have seemed like a normal Canadian conversation about the weather, but I knew there was more to it than that. I felt my parents were probing, an indirect longing to know more, to be on a more personal level.

The time had come to disclose my secret. "I won't need a car, Dad, because I don't expect to be here when winter comes."

By crossing this line, I gave my father an opportunity that he jumped at. "Your mother and I felt that you had some travel plans. Where do you plan to go?"

Now he caught me, because I was forced to give a direct and revealing answer. Instantly the cozy chair felt less comfortable, until I realized his question wasn't a trap. It was more a "wanting to know" from friends, two confidants that could be trusted with private information that I didn't know how to communicate. I knew that even though my parents didn't understand, they would listen without attacking me.

Taking a deep breath, I blurted out, "I am going to Israel to work on a *kibbutz!*" I was surprised it came out so directly.

"A 'key' what?" my Father exclaimed.

A heavy silence descended on the living room, and it seemed as if everyone held their breath.

My father broke the silence with a surprising remark, "Wow! You will really learn a lot from a trip like this."

On the surface this seemed like a simple response, but later I was to discover that his reaction had been deeply prophetic. Of course now they wanted to know everything, so I told them about the Israeli *shaliach* and the application process in Toronto. Besides giving a rough estimate on when I would be leaving, I didn't say more because they had received enough shocking news for one day.

How was I to explain my other feelings about God, the Holocaust and my interest in the beginning of Israel's history?

No, I decided. *They've had enough for now, we can deal with each question as it comes.*

CHAPTER 7

Saying Good-bye

Later that week Shaul informed me about a *kibbutz* that had accepted me, and I was expected to start the *ulpan* by mid-January. That was only a month and half away!

The pace of the journey towards Israel had begun like a gentle walk, now I felt like I was running. *Do I really know what I am doing?* This was the reoccurring question.

All those strange things which I had done this year happened in my own country, but my next steps were to be taken in a country I had only read about or heard about from others who had been there.

Feeling scared and excited at the same time, I had to keep my cool and not let it show. By now, the news of my travel plans had circulated amongst family members and friends. In the course of saying good-bye, I gradually learned about the mixed feelings and statements of what they thought of my plans.

"I don't understand how you can endanger your life!" was the most common reaction. "There are a lot of safer places you can go to. Why Israel?"

"If you're looking for a good cause to fight for, why not help the Indians on the reserves up in Northern Ontario?"

"Why the Heebs? You'll be given a return trip in a body bag."

Thankfully, my parents, who seemed to understand why I had to go, encouraged me in their own gentle way, and when my worried sister and brother-in-law realized that I wasn't going to change my mind, they decided to "wait and see."

In the course of time, Shaul the *shaliach* and I had become friends. After he learned I wasn't Jewish, his response had been, "Israel is for you also, you are welcome." I liked him because he had a direct way of speaking and was always to the point.

Many Westerners would perceive this as rude, but I liked his edginess. Being straightforward and honest didn't leave room for guessing what he really meant.

My last trip to the community center was to say good-bye to Shaul and thank him for all his help. We shook hands, and when I turned to leave he said, "Rick, I know you are interested in the Holocaust. There is a movie that is based on a true story from that period. It plays at a theater on the Danforth, downtown."

This was an area of Toronto about ten subway stops from the community center, but I had planned to go home, watch some TV and get to bed early in order to be fresh for work. This had been my routine during the last three months, and I still had a month to go before leaving. So what about that movie Shaul had mentioned? *I'm not going to a movie by myself,* I debated.

But today had been special. I had all the necessary papers, contact names on the *kibbutz*, even directions and bus numbers to take from the airport in Israel. Being assigned to *Kibbutz Ramat Hakovesh*, which meant "Hill of the Conqueror', I felt like I had conquered something myself, but wasn't sure what that was. At the Danforth subway stop, I jumped out and decided to celebrate by doing something different: after grabbing a quick hamburger, I was going to see the movie, alone. Walking along the street I noticed a large illuminated sign reading, "Pape Street Theater features *The Hiding Place* ." Since this was the only theater in that area on the Danforth, I figured this had to be the right place.

Shaul had not known the title of the movie, only that it had something to do with the Holocaust. At the entrance of the theater was a poster advertising the film with a picture of German soldiers pushing people into a truck. In the background was a large looming swastika. During the half hour before the next performance, images of the poster kept swirling through my head while I ate my hamburger and fries.

Since reading *Exodus*, I had read more books about the Holocaust, like *QB7* also by Leon Uris and *Mila 18*. For someone who had never really read a book before, the books by Leon Uris opened up a whole new world before me. Those books helped me to understand that the Holocaust had been a terrible "door" for the Jews. Entering that door gave birth to the State of Israel. Somehow, this God, whoever He was, or is, made this happen. Somehow He was involved.

Wondering if this movie would show me something else about this terrible door, I bought my ticket and slipped in just before the movie was about to start. It still felt a little strange being there by myself, but the feeling quickly passed.

The story of *The Hiding Place*, having taken place in Nazi occupied Holland during the Second World War, primarily focused on an elderly father and his two middle-aged, spinster daughters. These devout Christians saw their faith interwoven with the Jews and their struggles during the war. Father ten Boom, Corrie and Betsy understood that by aligning themselves with the Jews, they endangered their own lives along with everything they owned.

Despite the risks involved they created a hiding place for the Jews in their home, not because of superior religious arrogance, but because they felt it a privilege to do so. Despite their differences, they believed Jews and Christians belonged together. Later I also learned that there had been many Jews who had been trapped in life and death situations, but that there had been very few Christians who felt responsible to help them. These three people, who had been hiding Jews, were betrayed and arrested by the Gestapo. Thankfully, when the ten Boom family was arrested, the Jews in hiding were not found and later were able to escape.

Father ten Boom died in prison, and the two sisters were sent to a concentration camp where they suffered the same hell that had been created for the Jews. Betsy didn't survive the ordeal; through a miracle, Corrie was released. These three people had practiced their faith by giving their lives for the Jews, not by pious words, but by action. Compared to the sleeping Christian majority around them, the ten Booms seemed to act almost alone.

I will never forget a particular scene in the movie. A pastor tried to warn the family, convince them to stop helping the Jews. Father ten Boom argued, "The Jews are the Chosen People, the apple of God's eye!"

"They are the ones who killed Christ!" the pastor exclaimed.

At that moment one of the sisters entered the room holding a Jewish baby wrapped in a bundle of clothes. Noticing the pastor, she exclaimed, "Oh, Pastor! You are an answer to our prayers. You live in the country. This baby would be safe with you!"

The pastor declined to help the baby using the excuse that the child could endanger his life and that of his family. "Besides, Christians should obey the law," he stated. In haste he left the house.

"How can this man call himself a Christian?" Corrie fumed.

"Finding a mouse in the cookie jar doesn't make him a cookie," the father responded.

After watching the movie, I thought, *Somehow, we are defined by our actions and not by our religious titles.* Even though my parents took me to church when I was young I didn't know much about Christianity, let alone the denomination we belonged to.

Attending the services had been a test in endurance which I failed most of the time. Even as a child, I was able to discern the deep level of boredom on the faces of the adults and knew that they were also trying to "behave". Within Christianity there seemed to be a desire to be good in a religious sense, not due to a relationship. The only action I saw in religion demanded attending a service on a given day, not an action that could cost you your life.

The movie mentioned, "the apple of God's eye" or the "Chosen People" or "Christ Killers". As I began to understand more about the Holocaust, I learned that the European world had mainly focused on this third definition for the Jews, "Christ Killers".

On the way home all these thoughts whirled through my tired brain. The Jews, the Holocaust, and Israel – everything had so many aspects and each additional area that I was introduced to seemed to create more questions. Finally at the end of this very long day, the only question that I could deal with was, "How long until I can lay my head on my pillow?"

CHAPTER 8

The Last Christmas at Home

During my last month at work, it seemed that those who knew I was leaving for Israel became more anxious. Because it was Christmas time, I saw a lot of family and friends and noticed that people were giving me longer looks than normal. *They probably think this will be the last time they will see me alive,* I thought. *They are trying to imprint my face in their memory.* Many were probably also hoping I would change my mind at the last minute and "help the Indians" instead of that crazy Israel thing.

My flight was on January 7, 1977. Alone in my room I often checked and rechecked my airline ticket and passport, also to just look at them. Tuesday afternoon British Airways would fly me to London, then on Wednesday morning, after a three-hour layover, I was to catch the flight to Tel Aviv.

Celebrating Christmas was a good distraction for me. To me, it was always a favorite holiday in which we told stories, bought presents and talked about anything and everything.
Once the New Year's parties were behind us and everyone had recuperated from drinking too much alcohol, the days seemed to move fast. The approaching departure date gave me moments of anxiety but generally I was calm, experiencing a deep peace within.

The mood of my family and friends, however, was becoming more and more somber.
"We're coming to the airport to see you off!" friends and some family members told me. Inwardly I groaned, because I preferred to have only my parents and sister saying good-bye. This would be my first international flight, and I had to concentrate on what I was doing at the airport.

At the best of times I didn't like crowds, let alone becoming the center of attention for an audience, especially for a group who acted as if I was staging my own funeral. That would be the heavy part; in paradox, the flight to Israel would be the easy part.

One of my Christmas presents had been a new backpack, so on the evening before my departure I made sure every pocket was filled with what I thought I would need for the coming year. My carry-on had a few items I needed during the long flight, like the hardcover diary sketchbook my aunt had given me as a present. For as long as I can remember I had always been able to draw well, with my dear aunt being my biggest cheerleader.
I'm going to enjoy this sketchbook, I thought. *Surely there will be plenty of unsuspecting models on this trip.*

That night I didn't sleep well. Both my parents had taken the day off, therefore we had lots of time together the next morning. My mom made me a huge breakfast and an elaborate lunch, so by the time we got into the car, I was so full that I wouldn't have to eat anything during the flight. She probably did it on purpose: so that I would remember home a little longer.

CHAPTER 9

Airport Drama

As we drew closer to the airport, the atmosphere in the car grew heavier. We tried to make small talk at first but had fallen silent by the time we reached the airport. I was relieved to get out of the car.

The small crowd waiting at departures looked happy to see me. Wishing I could have said the same about seeing them, I felt their eyes on my back during check-in. All eyes went down when I dropped my passport. Hemmed in, I anxiously looked for the right gate while at the same time nodding to well-meaning people giving me a last piece of advice or a warning. Once I passed through the large glass door to passport control and to the gates, I had reached the point of no return. I longed to be alone, where no one would pay attention to me. Together with my fellow travelers I wanted to enter that place of peaceful self-absorption.
Almost there! Standing in front of the glass doors, I turned around to look at my friends and family standing in a semi-circle. Now came the last hurdle, the hardest one, when everyone waited uncomfortably for that last handshake, the last word, a final joke and the last punch in the shoulder.

Finally, I stood in front of the last person – my mother. I will never forget the way she looked at me. Without uttering a word, my mother communicated everything she wanted to tell me through her eyes. Cupping my face in her hands, she then hugged me so tight it almost hurt. As we both were trying very hard to be brave, she reached in her handbag and pressed a small book into my hand.
Without looking, I slipped it in my carry-on. Another hug. One last time we looked deeply into each other's eyes and nodded wordlessly. This was one of the deepest, most wordless conversations I ever had with my Mom.

"Bye everyone!" I waved. "I promise to write!" Quickly I headed for the doors, still feeling their eyes, but also a sense of relief. Another few waves and I was out of sight. Alone. Finally.

It was a relief to relax in one of the lounge chairs after the ordeal of saying good-bye. Now I could allow myself to become excited about the unknown journey ahead of me. While waiting to board the plane, I did not have enough time to do some sketching; but while rummaging through my bag to find something to eat, I touched the little book my Mom had given me. Remembering the look on her face when she gave it to me, I lingered for a few seconds before taking it out.
A New Testament? I thought. *What's this all about?* I almost laughed when I thought what my Mom had tried to tell me by giving me this.
"You are about to meet your Maker. We think He might have something to do with this book, so you better check it out".
Everyone went too far with their worrying, I thought. *If anyone sees me reading this, they'll think I'm some kind of religious nut.*

It was time to board the plane. *How do I get through this nine hour flight to London?* I wondered and began by taking out the snacks from my bag. Again, my hand touched the New Testament. I pulled it out. Carefully, I turned it over in my hand and noticed that the small book looked used and its corners were damaged. With no one sitting next to me I had the courage to leaf through it. *I'll just look through it for a while,* I told myself and actually felt curious.
When I began to read small portions about Jesus and some of the things He had said and done, I felt drawn to Him in a strange way. The experience was similar to when I had first read *Exodus,* but this time it wasn't about a country or a people, it was about a Man.
I felt drawn to this person, to His words, His actions, astounded by the way His friends recorded His character. While He had authority He was also gentle, and the fact that He was always approachable surprised me. Longing to know more about Him, I was happy to have all those hours to read.

My first reaction was, *This isn't real, I'm just reading history!* However, I sensed that the words He had spoken then were also present tense, that they had something very "now" about them.

As a young boy I had learned things about Jesus in church, but what I now read was totally new to me. Again, another mystery confronted me, triggering more questions which I had to examine.

Already I encountered many new personalities and mysteries: Israel, the Holocaust, Jews and now this Jesus - it all seemed to be woven together. Somehow I knew that all of this would be waiting for me in Israel.

Looking back over the past thirty years can be compared with looking at a wide horizon, searching for markers that can explain how I arrived at the point where I am now. On this journey, two beacons stand out clearly: the book *Exodus* and the Bible. Both old and nearly forgotten, they came into my life at a crucial turning point.

The "personality" of the Holocaust emerging from the book *Exodus* intersected with the personality of Jesus, emerging from the pages of the New Testament.

I was heading to the only country in the world that so prominently housed the remembrance of these two figures in history. However, I wasn't yet prepared for the conflict existing between the two of them.

Still, after all these years, I am amazed at how God wove the circumstances in such a marvelous way.

Ben Gurion Airport - Tel Aviv

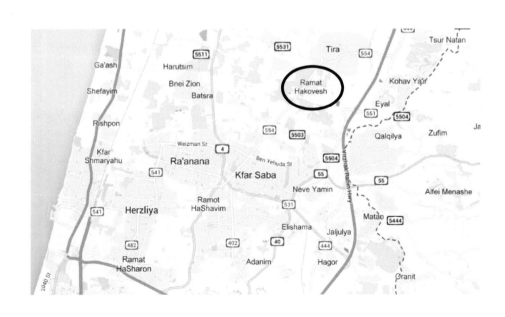

CHAPTER 10

Welcome to Israel!

During the three-hour layover in London, I pulled out my sketch book and began looking for unsuspecting models. Everything was new to me, and I noticed the airport was full of people rushing from one place to another. Amongst the travelers who had time to kill were many prospective models. I caught people in funny positions, especially when dozing off in uncomfortable, plastic airport chairs. They featured in some pretty interesting sketches I made.

During the four-hour flight from London to Tel Aviv, the passenger sitting next to me was a young guy with long hair and a beard. Except for the fact that he came from London and spoke with a Cockney accent, we could have been twin brothers. He talked almost the whole flight. I managed to respond with a word or a nod of my head at the appropriate moment, but had a difficult time understanding him. Somebody once joked that the British and the North Americans were two people groups that were separated by the same language.

From my window seat I saw Israel's shoreline appear, then we were flying over the country's largest city, Tel Aviv. The unfolding panorama moved me, but at the same time I wondered, *How am I to get to my kibbutz?*

"How do I get to Ramat Hakovesh?" I asked the girl at the information counter. "How much will it cost me to get there by taxi?"
I was dog-tired and decided to give myself a treat by taking a taxi. Having been a cab driver myself, I knew it was important to know the local prices so they couldn't take advantage of a travel-weary tourist who was new to the country.

After negotiating my ride with one of the clamoring drivers waiting outside the airport, I was off. During the one-hour drive to Ramat Hakovesh, I was pleased to find that the roads were paved and that everything was more modern than I had expected.

Driving through small towns, I tried to spot something familiar amongst all the new. The one thing I noticed was that the roof tops were flat, and each one had a rectangular, glass reflector next to a large, round, metal tank. I soon learned that these units were solar water heaters. Most of the buildings were constructed from either stone or poured concrete blocks; only a few had red, peeked roofs, tiled with ceramic. Then came the citrus orchards, full of colorful fruits and bordered by tall, dusty, cedar trees looking like sentinels.

"Kfar Saba" the road sign read in Hebrew and English. I knew this was the last town we would pass through before arriving at Ramat Hakovesh. As we drove closer I saw vast orchards along plowed fields, stretching out to the horizon on either side of the road.
Entering through the electric gate of the kibbutz, I saw long, narrow, single-story buildings with beautiful, green lawns with trees between them.

"Shalom, good luck!" the driver said after I paid him and pulled away. For a moment I stood there alone.
On my way to one of the buildings, a woman suddenly appeared. With a heavy, Israeli accent she said, "You look new."
"I am."
"Shalom! I'm Beila," she said, "the volunteer coordinator." She invited me into her makeshift office in one of the buildings and asked for my name and passport. "Sit down." Without asking if I wanted coffee, she handed me a cup, making me feel very welcome. Beila took me to the room I was to share with two other volunteers. Paul was a 25 year-old, quiet and moody Jew from New York and a chain smoker. Ian, on the other hand, was a friendly, Jewish South African. This good-looking guy was a real hit with the ladies. The room was exactly the length of two single beds put end to end. Next to Paul's bed stood a three-foot square plywood table, and our communal clothes closet stood on the other side of Ian's bed, which looked like a disaster site. I wondered how he managed to find enough space to sleep amongst all those dirty clothes piled up beside it.
Paul's corner was always neat as a pin, almost scary, while mine was somewhere in between.

Because my bed was beside the door, I couldn't spill over too much, or my stuff would block the door.

I acclimated to my surroundings in the few days before the start of *ulpan, the* Hebrew class that would last six months. There were about thirty students in the beginner's class, *kitah alef,* and twenty more advanced students in *kitah beth.* My first week was filled with strange new words. Learning the alphabet made me feel like a child again. It was the only way to survive a new language.

My classmates originated from about ten different countries. Some had been pressured by their families to volunteer on a kibbutz, others came because of community expectations, and a few were looking for adventure before making any serious life decisions. Considering Israel as a possible future was a common denominator for all of them. The other Gentile in my class was a Japanese guy who had "escaped" university in Japan to travel around in the Middle East.

The atmosphere in class was always charged with cultural differences, accompanied by floating and fluctuating desires whether to learn the language or not. The interaction fascinated me. Even though I was looking for God at the same time, I enjoyed the opportunity to be amongst all these different personalities.

Kibbutz

Ramat haKovesh

CHAPTER 11

Lost and Found in Haifa

By the end of our first week in *ulpan* everyone looked forward to our first *Shabbat* in Israel. Class finished early on Friday to give us a chance to travel elsewhere before the buses stopped running. On Saturday (Shabbat) evening, when public transportation started again, we were required to head back to the kibbutz for work and school on Sunday, the beginning of a new week in Israel.

As a way to encourage us to exercise our Hebrew, the teacher asked each of the students what we were planning to do on our day off. Thankfully there were a few classmates ahead of me, so there was time to rehearse my first public statement in Hebrew. It made me nervous, and I already felt embarrassed. *Ani nosa'ah laYerushlayim,* I repeated over and over in my mind. (I'm going to Jerusalem). By the time my turn came, different cities and towns had been named as destinations. Red-faced and perspiring, I managed to say the right words, sat back and listened to the nervous attempts of the others.

The last one was a girl from New York who said, "*Ani nosa'at la Haifa*" (I am traveling to Haifa.) And then, for no reason at all, she called,
        "Rick! Some of us are catching a ride with a van to Haifa. Wanna join us? There's one seat left."
It was a strange request, especially after I had just told the class that I was going to Jerusalem. However, this girl, whom I didn't know well, now offered me a ride to Haifa. *Maybe He wants me to go to Haifa,* I thought. *I would be going to Haifa anyway sometime, so why not now?*
        "Sure I'll join you," I called back.

Haifa is a port city on the Mediterranean with the Carmel mountain range rising up almost immediately from the seashore dividing the city into two parts, the lower "Hadar", and the upper 'Carmel."

We reached the city early Friday evening, yet by that time it was already dark and raining lightly. *Glad I brought my winter coat,* I thought. The army green coat had a large hood and at least ten large pockets; some I had filled with bread and vegetables from the kibbutz. January in Israel is often cold and wet —"cold" being a relative term for a

Canadian, for Israeli cold is between 40 to 50 degrees Fahrenheit (5-10 degrees Celsius).

The driver stopped the van in front of the central bus station, and I got out thinking that the others would join me. To my surprise, the door closed and the van drove off! Everywhere I looked was wet and dark, except for city lights high up in the distance. There was hardly any traffic. and I felt utterly alone. *I better get a map of the city, but where?* I nervously thought.

Quickly walking across the street to the bus station I was just in time to buy a map at a newspaper stand before it closed.

"Which bus do I take into the city?" I asked the owner.

"It's Shabbat, there are no buses," he said.

"Do you know if there is a youth hostel nearby?"

"No," was all he said before quickly walking away.

What am I going to do now? I wondered. *At least I have a map, and I can always find a park to sleep in.*

I thought like a Canadian – imagining parks with soft lawns and wide trees to cover a person against the rain. Soon I realized that was not possible for Haifa in winter.

Standing at the intersection, while debating which direction to choose, I softly said, "I thought *You* wanted me to come here. Well, here I am. Now what? Which way?" Nothing dramatic happened.

I'll turn right and head for the upper part of the city, I thought. *I'm a tourist. This way I can take a look at the city lights.*

Walking in the direction of the upper Carmel, I stopped one of the few taxis to ask the driver, "Do you know of a youth hostel here?"

"Yes, we have a government hostel just outside the city," the man responded. "I'll be happy to take you, but because it's *Shabbat* the price is triple the usual fare," he warned.

Unable to afford the ride, I trudged through streets congested with tall

apartment buildings. By now all the shops were closed.

I finally reached the top of the mountain range, where there were several small terraced parks, expensive shops and a row of fancy hotels.

I sat down on a bench overlooking the scenic Haifa Bay.

On the distant coastline even the oil refineries sparkled. Though I enjoyed the view, I still didn't have a place to sleep. It was getting late, and my coat was wet and heavy from the rain.

"I thought You wanted me to come," I said again. "Here I am, I don't have a place to stay, and I barely know where I am right now." It wasn't a prayer, more a statement. Not knowing what else to do, I decided to return to the lower city.

On my way down I bumped into a pedestrian who spoke English, so I asked him about a hostel. He didn't know of any in the area, but suggested, "There is the Scandinavian Seaman's Home just a little further down the street. Pretend you are a sailor and maybe they will

give you a room for the night."
Desperate, I was willing to do anything. Following the man's directions, ten minutes later I rang the bell of the Seaman's Home and told the lady about my predicament.

"No, I'm sorry, you can't stay here," she told me. As I was about to walk away, she called me back. "Wait! There's an American couple living across the street who sometimes take people in for the night." Even though this sounded a bit strange to me, I was willing to give it a try and rang the bell on the iron gate of the two-story building.
Nobody answered. Suddenly I noticed a small note in English, "When we don't answer this door, please use the side door."
After I rang the bell at the side door, it was opened by a middle aged woman.

"Is it true that you take in people for the night?" I asked uncomfortably.

"Of course! Do you need a bed?"
Surprised by her friendliness, I mumbled, "Yes please. If that's possible."

"Come in, but we have a meeting going on right now."
I stepped inside before she could suggest otherwise.
What does she mean by a "meeting"? I had no idea and didn't care, as long as I was out of the cold and in a warm and dry room.
Taking my drenched coat, the woman gave me a towel to dry off my face and brought me to the living room which was full of people.

It was strange, seeing all these young and older people there. Someone took a guitar, another called out the number on the song sheet, and everyone joined in the singing. Feeling awkward, I just listened to the peaceful melody while reading the words on the paper I received. All the songs on the sheet were about Jesus; it was as if they were talking to Him through the music. *Maybe it was Him who brought me to Haifa. Maybe all these strange things had to happen for me to sit here tonight.* The thought shocked me. Even though I didn't know anybody in this room, I felt as if I belonged.

After the singing ended, a man introduced himself as Wilbur. "That's my wife, Betty." He pointed to the woman who invited me in.

"Thank you all for coming," Wilbur said. "I'd like to give a short teaching from the New Testament."

I was drawn, for I was familiar with the New Testament from my reading on the plane. *This is no accident that I have come to this place,* I began to realize. The same God that I had been trying to find was beginning to be found – amazing! After Wilbur finished speaking, he prayed and closed the meeting. A few girls who volunteered with them had prepared some snacks and drinks. We began to mingle and talk. The conversation was casual, and everyone was warm and friendly.

Later that evening Betty handed me a set of sheets with a blanket and showed me where I could sleep. The room looked like a dorm or a hostel with bunk beds.

"We have breakfast at eight tomorrow morning," Betty told me.

On *Shabbat* morning I joined the other guests at the long table in the dining room, but before we could start our simple breakfast, they sang a song. It was like a blessing over the food, and it touched me deeply. For so many years I had never even been awake at this hour on a Saturday morning. My usual wake-up time was past noon, accompanied by a bad headache with blurred memories of the night before. Being up this early and singing a blessing over my food was foreign to me. However, I actually liked it.

Arthur Blessitt in Jerusalem, 1977

CHAPTER 12

Meeting Arthur Blessitt

From that time on I regularly traveled to Haifa for the weekends to stay at the hostel on Hagefen Street. It was wonderful getting to know the people and listening to their stories or testimonies of how they had come to faith in Jesus.

One of the weekends I decided to go to Jerusalem instead. With my tourist map I walked through the ancient, clustered alleys inside the Old City. The coolness of the stone walls, bells ringing, voices of buyers and vendors, all those strange exotic smells were exciting; it was like experiencing a rich living history. The name of the city, Jerusalem, was interwoven in many a Biblical story as a connecting point between God and His ancient People.
On my way to the Mount of Olives I got lost.
"Can you tell me how to get there?" I asked a passerby.
"Just follow this street, the Via Dolorosa," the man told me.
The name sounded familiar.

Suddenly I heard loud, excited voices. Singing people accompanied a sun tanned man wearing a T-shirt, jeans and sandals. The most surprising thing was that he carried a life-size wooden cross. Smiling broadly, the man maneuvered the heavy cross through the busy *shuk*. I decided to follow the crowd, to see what this was all about.
The man halted in front of the Church of the Redeemer, a Lutheran church. Standing on a chair, he spoke about Jesus, what He meant to him personally. Then he prayed.
When I closed my eyes, it was as if a blanket fell, as if I was wrapped in a secure embrace.
"I'll be sharing more about my walk with this cross at the Garden Tomb," the man said. "You are all welcome to join us."

Having no idea where he was headed I tagged along behind until we came to a beautiful, quiet, walled-in garden.

The Garden Tomb, I discovered, was the traditional Protestant site of the crucifixion and the burial of Jesus. It was located near one of the busiest sections of the city, not far from the touristic hub outside the walls of the Old City.

Sitting unnoticed in the last row of chairs, I listened to Arthur Blessitt's experiences of carrying his cross through many different countries.

"The reason I've been carrying this cross for so many years is because I follow Jesus," he explained. "My relationship with Jesus is now, present tense, and real to the degree that I am willing to carry this cross in so many strange places in obedience to this relationship. Jesus is King over my life."

Deep inside of me something responded to his words. I didn't want to be king over my life any longer. Before this journey to Israel had begun, my life had been a mess. There, in the Garden Tomb, I quietly gave my life to Jesus, for Him to rule my life instead of me.

"If You make Your will known to me and if I'm sure it is You, I will do it, whatever you ask of me. I will let You rule."

The moment I whispered these words a weight was lifted off me.

All the way back to the Central Bus Station, I had a deep sense of peace. In a way, it was the end of the search but the beginning of a life that would be more than anything I could ever have imagined.

CHAPTER 13

Kibbutz Life

The kibbutz members were always very kind to me; it didn't bother them that I wasn't Jewish. Especially the older ones, knowing I didn't have family in Israel, they did their best to make me feel welcome. There seemed to be a special place in their hearts for "orphans". Spending my free afternoons drinking cups of coffee and enjoying homemade cake, I found out why by listening to their stories on how they came to Israel and the kibbutz. The founding fathers and mothers of Ramat Hakovesh had come to Israel in their late teens and early twenties. These Polish Zionist youth group members established the kibbutz. Most of them came from large Jewish families that hoped to follow their sons and daughters to what was known then as Palestine. Unfortunately, when the Second World War broke out, many of those family members became trapped in Europe and were eventually mur-dered by the Nazi regime. As a result of the Holocaust, many kibbutz members had become orphans and, therefore, were able to identify with those of us who were without family in the country.

Ramat haKovesh in the early days

They told me their stories and saw that I was fascinated with their history. I asked many questions, but then one day they asked me something personal. "What brought you to Israel?"
Deciding to be honest with them, I told them about my search for God and how I had met Jesus during my first months of living in Israel.
I remember clearly the look on their faces when I mentioned His name – Jesus. It was as if I had used a swear word. *Why*? I wondered.

"Let me tell you what this name means to us Jews," my friends began. "Throughout the ages, we have been blamed for His death. The Christian Church looks upon us as if we are a lesser people, a cursed people deserving to be punished." I later learned about the Crusades, the Inquisition and the Pogroms; the church always felt it to be their responsibility to punish the Jews for what "they had done in crucifying Jesus". The Orthodox Church in Poland and the Ukraine was overly zealous around Christmas and especially around Easter time, when they would kill, rape and plunder each and every Jew they could find.
Many of the older kibbutz members agreed that the church had caused most of their suffering as a people. This persecution of Jews accumulated over hundreds of years of European history, ending with the horrific atrocities of the Holocaust. Hearing their version created a big dilemma for me. Knowing more about the dark history of the church, I could understand why they felt the way they did, but the person of Jesus that I was just getting to know didn't match their perception of Him. I began to realize that the church institution that claimed Jesus as their Lord didn't reflect who He truly had been.

I came to love the life style on the kibbutz – not only the interaction with the people, also the hard, physical work in the fields. Deciding to stay a bit longer on the kibbutz had its merits, for my "seniority" entitled me to a private room. Returning from the fields one day, my eyes fell on a pile of discarded branches of avocado trees, and I carried an interesting, large piece of gnarled wood to my room. I began to carve the wood in my spare time with just a simple knife. Realizing the wood was too hard for a regular knife, I asked the carpenter on the kibbutz if I could borrow some old chisels and a mallet.

I don't really know why, because I had never done wood carving before. Sure, I knew how to draw and paint, but artistically this was totally different. There was plenty of free time, so the moment my work in the banana plantation was done, I continued to carve in the wood. I didn't have anything specific in mind, but studying the wood, I imagined seeing certain shapes which I tried to "free" with the chisels.

Feeling the tools in my hand and shaping the wood was a type of meditation, a place for my thoughts to explore. I kept pulling out what I "saw". Here, I saw two hands together, and there, within that rough bark, I saw a face and then a single eye. It didn't really matter if it made sense or not; just the feel, the smell and the interaction with the tools in the carving of the wood. Sometimes after work, I planned to carve for only a few minutes, take a shower and head for the dining room. More than once, though, I checked the clock to see if it really was past midnight, realizing I had been carving for hours! With only a few hours left before I had to get up again, I didn't even bother to Undress and just went to sleep in my work clothes.

Those of us studying in the *ulpan* were given an adoptive "family" from amongst the kibbutz members. The idea was that this would help us to use our Hebrew and learn more about life on the kibbutz. My adoptive family, the Carmis, were great. To this day we are in touch with them. Moti, my kibbutz father, was born on the kibbutz; both his parents had been able to leave Poland just before the war started in 1939. Ruti, my kibbutz mom, was born on a nearby kibbutz. Both her Hungarian-born parents had survived the horrors of the Holocaust.

When I first arrived, Zohar, the Carmis' four year-old daughter, was the only one who had the patience to put up with my bad Hebrew. The other children were Dani, Noga and Zeev.
I tremendously appreciated the generosity of this wonderful family. Even though Ruti and Moti were only ten years older than me, the level of my conversational Hebrew always made me feel like a small child. Moti was quiet and more reserved, while Ruti had a strong personality with pronounced opinions on just about everything.

She told me exactly what she thought about God, how ridiculous it was for anyone to believe that such a "thing" existed. Bringing up the subject of my faith in Jesus would infuriate her, so I kept quiet about it unless she brought it up.

After carving in the wood for about three months, I realized a pattern had developed. The different images I had carved in the wooden

 branch told the story of Jesus healing the blind man. Without any intention, they visually told the story. I was intrigued by it, for it was as if I had been able to express the story creatively, by drawing from the spiritual side of who I now was.

During all those hours of carving I had lost myself in work and thoughts. It had felt like a time of deep prayer, as if I had dug deep into myself to express something which now could be seen outwardly.

A few days later Ruti came by my place to check up on me, and like a good Mom she complained, "Your room is a mess! You need to clean up!" Noticing the carving in the middle of the room, she fell quiet and studied the details.

"How beautiful!" she exclaimed, obviously curious about the artwork. "When it's finished, it's mine!" she pointed to herself. "I already know where it will fit in my house."
Knowing that protesting would be futile, I only nodded.

It took me another few weeks before I felt the piece was ready.
For days, Ruti had been pestering me to finish the carving. Debating whether to tell her what I saw in the piece and what it meant to me, I knew Ruti would be angry about my story of Jesus. After praying for wisdom, I told her the piece was ready.

"Can you come tomorrow to my room to pick it up?"
When Ruti came the next day, I said, "I'd like to tell you what I see in the wood."

Sitting on the edge of my bed, for twenty minutes she listened to me telling the story of Jesus healing the blind man through the different images in the carved trunk. It was a miracle, for she never interrupted me even once!

"*Toda Raba,* Thank you," she said. "I think it's such a beautiful piece of art." She left with the carving in her arms.

Stunned, I felt the Lord speak to my heart and say, *This is your language to communicate to them.*

It was then that I began to discover that art provided me with an inner "language" that touched the heart without words.

Years later, long after my wife Dafna and I had left the kibbutz, we visited Moti and Ruti. I noticed that the sculpture which always stood in the far corner of the room was gone.

"What happened to the sculpture?" I asked Ruti cautiously.

"I decided to give it to my mother," she told me.

Aggie, who had come to Israel from Hungary after WWII, had always liked the sculpture. Ruti wanted her mother to have it in her home.

For many years she enjoyed the piece until her eyesight began to fail. At the age of 84, Aggie had become legally blind.

It always amazes me to think that the first piece of sculpture I ever did, communicating the story of Jesus healing the blind man, ended up for years in the home of a blind Holocaust survivor.

Aggie since then has passed away.

Left to right: Rick and Zoar, Moti (Kibbutz Father) Ruti and Dani (now 41 years old)
Front: Paul, a British volunteer who was a friend of mine then.

"For the LORD will have mercy on Jacob, and will yet choose Israel, and set them in their own land: and the strangers shall be joined with them, and they shall cleave to the house of Jacob."
Isaiah 14:1

CHAPTER 14

Isaiah 14

Travelling throughout the land, I met other believers from different nations and backgrounds. Some of them told me they had "heard" the voice of the Lord speak to them and what had happened after they obeyed. This fascinated me.

"Did you actually hear the Lord speak?" I wanted to know. "What does He sound like?" I wanted to know if this was real.

"When the Lord speaks, you just know it is Him," they told me. "You'll experience a deep peace within."

It sounded nice, but I needed something more tangible.

Ilona, a German volunteer on the kibbutz, and I became good friends. When she had to return to Germany to continue her schooling, we decided I would join her to meet her parents. Our relationship was becoming serious, and I was happy for it. My time in Israel had been very good, now I felt leaving for Germany should be the next step. One of my friends told me that unless I received a "word" from the Lord telling me to stay, I should leave Israel, because this was a difficult place for a young believer. It would be much easier for me in another country.

About three weeks before Ilona was scheduled to leave, a friend needed a place to sleep, so I offered my room. My kibbutz parents always let me use the couch in their living room, so I settled down for the night in their house. Around midnight, my head was filled with pleasant thoughts about my new adventure to Germany. Even though Israel would always have a special place in my heart, it seemed like the time had come to move on. While I was busy thinking and planning, another thought entered my mind, seemingly from nowhere. Uninvited, it pushed itself into my stream of thinking.

"Isaiah fourteen" was all the voice said. Nothing more.

Strange, I thought but ignored the intrusion by returning to my other, pleasant thoughts.

A few minutes later the voice repeated, stronger, "Isaiah fourteen!" I was at a loss of what to do. Being only a young believer, I knew that Isaiah was somewhere in my Bible, but I still didn't know where.

My Bible was in my backpack on the other side of the room, and I felt too comfortable in bed to get up and get it. Suddenly, I felt such an urgency that I forced myself to turn on the light and get my Bible.

It took me some time to find the book of Isaiah. Sitting on the edge of the couch I began to read the first verse of chapter fourteen.

>*"For the Lord will have mercy on Jacob, and will still choose Israel, and settle them in their own land. The strangers will be joined with them, and they will cling to the house of Jacob. Then people will take them and bring them to their place, and the house of Israel will possess them for servants and maids in the land of the Lord;"*

Reading those words, I immediately knew that I was one of the "strangers."

The returning or "settling" of the Jews in their own land had been the driving force that had brought the nation of Israel into being once again. By God's mercy they had been brought to their own homeland after the Second World War and the Holocaust. I didn't know that strangers could be attached to this land. When I returned to bed, there was a deep sense of God's "presence" in the room. However, this Bible verse triggered many questions.

Do You want me to stay in Israel, Lord? Am I one of these strangers who is being joined to this house and this land? Then I remembered what my believer friends had told me, that if the Lord had spoken, I would experience a deep peace. *Okay, Lord,* I thought. *If I stay in Israel, what will happen with Ilona? I don't think I'm going to have peace about that one.*

Wrapping myself in the blanket, I felt a strange peace come over me. Soon I was fast asleep.

The next morning I spoke with Ilona about what had happened to me during the night. Even though it all seemed rather strange, even mystic, I continued to feel a deep peace in my heart when I told her. I knew this would be hard for her to accept because she wanted me to come to Germany, hoping we would marry there. Yet, I had given my life to Jesus and wanted the reality of His Kingship in my life. Would this be a test of that reality? I had to respond, make a decision about what I could only describe as a strange, spiritual experience.

I could choose to shake off the voice I heard in the night, embrace my relationship with this beautiful German girl and go with her. To make real life decisions on the basis of spiritual promptings seemed extreme; it didn't seem stable. The bottom line was that if I wanted His Kingship in every area of my life, not only did I have to take this "prompting" seriously, I also had to find a way to respond to it somehow.

"This word you think is from the Lord needs to be confirmed or proved," Ilona reminded me.
She had a point. *But how do I confirm this?* I wondered. *What do I need to do?*
Suddenly an idea came to mind. *I'll go to the Ministry of Interior and apply for residency,* I decided. *If the Lord wants me to stay in Israel, I'll need to have that stamped in my passport.*

CHAPTER 15

Miracle at *Misrad haPnim*[1]

I knew that in Israel it was almost impossible for a non-Jew to apply for any type of residency status. This *will be a good way to check out this word,* I thought. *It's something I can't manipulate, so it either is from God or it isn't.*
There were four different kinds of statuses in Israel: after the tourists came the temporary residents, followed by the permanent residents, and the highest status would be that of citizens.

I went to the Ministry of Interior and asked for a meeting with the visa clerk. After waiting for a long time, I was finally summoned to an office. Behind a large, wooden desk in the middle of the room was a heavy-set, middle-aged woman who seemed to have been a clerk for a very long time, and not too happy about it.
I felt nervous, but had rehearsed what I was going to say.

"What do you need?" She sounded impatient.

"I would like to apply for temporary residency," I said.
Looking at me, she scowled. "Are you Jewish? No? Well, then it is not for you."

"I am aware of that, but I would like to apply anyway."
Surprised at my *chutzpah,* she repeated, "No! This status is not for you. It was nice of you to come to Israel for a visit, but you'll have to leave now. This is a Jewish State. If I send these papers to Jerusalem, they will surely refuse your request."

"I know that too, and really appreciate your help. It's only a form, a piece of paper. Let's fill it out anyway," I implored.
Noticing she began to squirm in her chair, I knew she was becoming angry. "Okay, well, if that is the case, why not apply for permanent residency? They will turn you down either way, so why not go straight for the biggest one?"

---

[1] Ministry of Interior

"All right, let's do that," I agreed, sensing I had wasted enough of her time and she wanted me out of her office.
As my Hebrew was still very basic, the woman helped me by filling out the forms.

Because I had to stay in the country to hear what the Ministry of Interior had decided about my status, I said good-bye to Ilona, promising to let her know as soon as possible if I would be coming to Germany. My feelings were mixed. On one hand, I wanted to deepen the relationship with her, but on the other hand, I wanted to know if my relationship with Jesus could be real.

While continuing to work on the kibbutz, I waited. As the weeks turned into months, I returned to the daily work rhythm which I enjoyed. Six months after my visa application, I found an official-looking letter from the Ministry of Interior in my postbox. I had almost forgotten about the application; therefore, the letter came as a surprise. At lunchtime in the dining room, I opened the envelope. Inside was a small piece of paper with only one Hebrew sentence: "Your request has been granted. Please bring in your passport to the nearest Interior office."
Not sure that I understood correctly, I went over and over the words.
"What does this mean?" I asked my kibbutz friends.
"It looks like whatever it was you asked for has been given to you." They smiled at me.
Feeling excited, at the same time I was filled with wonder. It wasn't just excitement in the sense of, "Wow, I can stay in Israel," but more like, "Wow! He really spoke to me! God speaks to us! He spoke and I actually understood Him!"

The next day I went to the Interior Ministry and again had to face the formidable woman. I wasn't sure if she remembered me, but being so happy with my slip of paper, I acted as if we were old friends.
"They gave it to me! They gave me permanent residency!"
Cheerfully I handed her the paper.
By then she probably remembered who I was and didn't seem particularly overjoyed to see me.

After reading the piece of paper, without looking at me, she crumpled it into a small ball and threw it in the wastebasket beside her desk.

"It's a mistake," was all she said before getting up and leaving the office.

Not knowing what to do, I debated whether to pick out my little slip of paper from the bin. *Is this the end of our meeting?* I wondered. *Why did she walk out?* All kinds of thoughts tumbled through my head. *How did I mess up? Does this mean the Lord didn't speak to me? Should I stay?* All my joy had evaporated.

Suddenly the door opened and in walked the woman with a big file in her hands. Without saying a word or looking at me, she sat down and slowly went through the papers.

After a while she looked at me. "I don't understand. There must be some kind of mistake," she mumbled.

I was surprised, but before I could say anything, she continued to check the papers, repeating to herself, "I just don't understand. They have given you permanent residency. How could this happen?"

Hope returned!

Trying to be sympathetic I said, "That is okay. You don't have to understand. All you have to do is stamp my passport, then I will leave. You will never have to see me again!"

"But I have never, ever seen this happen before!" she exclaimed.

Impatiently pushing my passport in her direction, I tried to appear calm. Finally, after what seemed like a very long time, she pulled a big rubber stamp from her drawer and with a loud "thump" stamped my passport with permanent resident status.

Deep emotions welled up in me. Controlling myself, I thanked her and walked out of the office.

Together with this feeling of great awe towards God, I also sensed my responsibility towards everything that just had transpired.

This moment had been a milestone, one that had the power to direct the rest of my life, for I could never say that this had not been God's doing. By receiving confirmation that I was to stay in Israel, this also meant that my relationship with Ilona had ended.

In the following months I began to ponder, *If I'm to stay here, then I must do what everyone else does, serve in the IDF.* I talked to several men on the kibbutz who helped me in getting accepted into the army. I was part of a small paratroopers unit, and I fought alongside my fellow soldiers in the First Lebanon War of 1981.

If someone had told me that four years after arriving in Israel I would be fighting in the Israeli army, I would have told him that he was crazy. God surpassed all my thoughts and imaginations!

After finishing my army service, I decided to apply for citizenship and received it without any problems. God has amazed me in how much He loves this people and this land. He allowed me to interact and identify through so many relationships.

I am truly thankful to Him - He is a great Father.

Israeli Defense Forces - Paratrooper Unit buddies

Chapter 16

Dafna's Story

I was born as Lori Scheimann in 1959 and grew up in Ft. Wayne, Indiana, with my parents and two brothers - I was the middle child. Both my parents were Lutheran, each having German ancestry. Their families had been living in the same area for at least three generations. I remember that my father's parents spoke German when they didn't want us to understand what was being said.

Life in the US was fairly normal with school, birthdays, holidays, and family camping vacations. On the outside we seemed like a loving family, but by the 1970's the hidden marital problems my parents had were leading them towards divorce, creating much unrest in our home. Even though the Lutheran church always had been a rock for my dad, he no longer found answers there and began looking elsewhere. At the time my mother was seeing a professional medical counselor. One evening, while watching a Billy Graham broadcast in our basement TV room, my Dad, desperately asking for help, called out to God. As a first step he seriously began to read the Bible and no longer went out socially drinking with his buddies. Noticing this change, my mother wondered if he, too, should see her counselor.

"No", my father explained. "I've changed because I'm now more focused on God."

"That is what I've been looking for all my life!" My mom was elated.

This happened in 1973 when the Charismatic Movement moved through America. My parents began to attend tent revivals, small home group meetings, and even Charismatic Catholic events. Despite the fact that my parents seemed happy, excited and focused on rebuilding their marriage, this sudden change distressed me. They even said they loved each other!
Is this for real? I wondered.

Unwilling to believe the change in them, I became rebellious and tried to live my own life by going in the opposite direction. For a period of three years I watched my parents and their friends.

"We love you," they always told me, "and we're praying for you."

Nice, I thought, *but I have my own friends who 'love' me.*

Towards the end of my third rebellious year, I made an effort to take a good look at myself. *Who am I?* I wasn't sure. *Am I the one who tries to be the 'good girl' at home in order to keep the peace? Or the one who is getting more and more into trouble when out with my friends?* Deep in my heart I knew that if something bad happened to me, my friends would not be able to help me because they were in the same mess as I was. On the other hand, knowing that my parents and their friends would accept me whatever the situation, I began to trust them more and more.

During their spiritual search my parents also discovered that the Bible was very Jewish. What are the holidays - Passover and Sukkoth? They wondered. Slowly, they began to understand that Israel was not an ancient story but that it was a living, vibrant, modern day state which they wanted to learn about and experience themselves. After visits to our Jewish neighbors and reading many books, my parents made a visit to the Israeli Embassy in Chicago, "Would it be possible to live in Israel?" they asked. It was suggested to my father to send his resume as an engineer in truck design to different companies in Israel. A company in Nazareth Illit responded by sending him a telegram saying they needed a truck engineer like him. Could he come within the year? After several more meetings at the Israeli Embassy my parents decided to sell everything we owned - house, cars, the lake cottage - and move to Israel.

By this time I was also ready to join them as I had given my life to the Lord and had made a commitment to follow Him. Moving to Israel would give me a new chance, a new beginning.

CHAPTER 17

First Encounter with Rick

We arrived in Jerusalem in September, 1976. Experiencing the Old and New City was awesome – there were so many new sounds, smells, new faces. It was a modern city living together with ancient history. Living with a group of Americans helped us to acclimate to the "Land". Three months later we moved to Afula in the Jezreel Valley to be closer to the company where my father was to work. It was also during this time I had changed to "Dafna". Lori is a derivative of Laurel which in Hebrew translates to Dafna. As a family we enrolled in *Ulpan* for six months to learn the Hebrew language. We made new friends by getting acquainted with the Jewish customs of our Tunisian and Moroccan neighbors. Whenever we could, we traveled around the country to enjoy the sights.

Haifa wasn't far from Afula, so on Fridays we often drove to a youth hostel where a small group of believers met together. A young Canadian named Rick Wienecke would also come to these meetings and stay overnight at the hostel. He was a new believer in Jesus, totally in love with Israel, and his only desire was to know more of both. When I first saw him, he had long, wavy, sand-colored hair and a bushy beard. His checkered shirt along with blue "overall" jeans were his "best clothes", they were also to become his trademark at that time. It was his easy-going, friendly smile that caught my attention. As a result of my previous years I had become reserved; shy at eighteen years old, I found it difficult to make random conversation even with people my own age. It was my father who had struck up several conversations with Rick and discovered they both played tennis. He invited Rick to our home on Friday nights so they could play tennis on *Shabbat* mornings.

Rick and I became friends; I enjoyed it when he came, because he was clever, funny and made me laugh. As the years went by, both Rick and I had other friends and some serious relationships. I had a strong relationship with an Israeli young man whose family I had grown fond of during our first two years in Afula. Later, a handsome Dutchman wanted me to visit him in Holland. Regardless of our other interests, Rick and I stayed in contact with each other. It was always easy to sit and talk with him because we had a natural and friendly concern for each other.

I loved my job as a nursery school assistant. Being with the 2-4 year olds teaching them songs and stories, I learned a lot myself, particularly about the Jewish culture, the holidays, history and attitudes. I enjoyed working on the children's art projects, the plays and their birthday parties. Knowing it wasn't to be my future as a *Ganenet* (nursery teacher), I decided to enroll in nursing school in 1979.

Afula has a large hospital for the whole area including the Arab villages, *kibbutzim*, and *moshavim*. Despite the fact that the nursing school adjacent to the hospital was close to our home, I opted to live in the student dormitories. This way I was able to study with the other girls, as I was still learning Hebrew as a second language. During this time I focused on my student life and at the same time looked forward to my future as a nurse.

In the meantime Rick had gone to a religious kibbutz for a three-month course on Judaism. Even though we did not see much of each other, we kept in touch.

In 1980, when Rick was 26 years old, he joined the IDF and became a paratrooper in a unit named *Shaked* (almond). Around the same time I decided to leave Afula and continue my training at the smaller hospital in Poriah near the Sea of Galilee. I became a licensed nurse in 1981. While working on the maternity and gynecology ward, I lived in one of the nurses' apartments on the hospital grounds.

I loved my profession but found the constant shift rotations to be very challenging.

CHAPTER 18

"You are my best friend ever..."

Rick and I had always stayed in contact and saw each other occasionally. At this time I noticed that Rick was phoning quite regularly, which made me wonder if he suddenly had become more interested in me. Because of my own busy life I didn't realize that it took quite an effort for him to make these phone calls. Cell phones didn't exist then, and his unit was constantly on the move. But I was always pleased to hear from my best friend. At one point I asked him, "Why are you phoning so often?" hoping to get more of a committed response to a relationship. He only gave me a casual remark.

Not long afterward Rick came to visit me at the nurses' apartment while dressed in his army uniform and carrying a large kit bag and I wore my nurse uniform. I was comfortable with Rick's visits, whether at my parent's home in Afula or during outings with friends. Usually we were relaxed in each other's company, but this time it was different. He was more serious, as if he had something on his mind. Sitting stiffly in the chair while I sat on the narrow bed in my room, Rick looked at me intently and said,

"I think our relationship is becoming more serious. What do you think?"
I was shocked! This was a direct question, in person, exactly what I had wanted to hear, but at the same time I struggled with thoughts like, *but what about my job? These crazy shifts, how will I manage to commit to both?*

"Rick," I said, "You are my best friend ever! We can be friends."

In my mind this was a show of my trust in him, and hoped this would open the door for more discussion. However, to my surprise, Rick nodded and said, "I think it's time for me to go." He then picked up his bag and went to the door.

His reaction alarmed me. This wasn't like Rick! Standing on the porch of the apartment to say good-bye, I noticed the golden sunset, like in the movies, when a guy is saying goodbye for the last time.

"Does this mean you won't be phoning me as much?" I asked. Throwing his kit bag over his shoulder Rick said, "Is there a reason I should?" He walked off into the sunset to catch a ride to his army base, far up North.

Distraught, I realized that Rick had misunderstood me. He thought my words meant that I was not interested in a relationship deeper than friendship. Right then, I knew that if I didn't do something, I was going to lose someone very precious.

Sometimes on the weekends, when I was free from hospital duty, I would either go to my parent's house or take the bus to "Beit Emanuel", a Messianic youth hostel not far from the Tel Aviv beach. Young believers between the ages of 18 -30 would meet on Saturday nights for bible teaching, worship music, and just "hang out" time. Knowing Rick would be there the next weekend, I asked my roommate to French-braid my shoulder-long hair. Choosing my best shirt and slacks, I packed an overnight bag and headed for Tel Aviv. I had to talk to Rick! Tell him what I really felt!

I arrived in time for the evening gathering only to find Rick talking with friends, who were girls! The whole evening I made sure to stay close to him. We joined a group of friends for a late pizza that night and I was sad to notice that Rick was friendly but reserved towards me. When I found out he had booked a bed at the hostel dorms, I was glad I had decided to do the same.

The next morning there were only a few people at the breakfast table, so we had a good opportunity to talk.

"Its my day off from the base", Rick said "I have some errands to do in the city."

"Can I join you?" I asked.

Together we took the bus to the old city of Yaffo to the nearest Licensing bureau. While standing in line with Rick I was busy thinking, *When would be a good time to talk to him? Not on the bus. No, impossible and we can't talk here either.* I decided to wait for the right moment.

Time was passing by too quickly. I had to be back in Poriah in time for my night shift. The bus ride would take almost three hours to get there. When Rick offered to walk me to the Central Bus Station in Tel Aviv, this encouraged me as I felt things were warming up again.

The route via the beach meant climbing down a rather steep hill of rugged, large rocks. Elated, I grabbed Rick's hand when he helped me down and didn't let go even when we had reached the beach.

I was beginning to feel I could finally say the words to let him know how I felt about our relationship.

We sat down on the warm sand. That early autumn day the weather was balmy with a mild ocean breeze. I so much enjoyed just being with Rick that I almost forgot to make my speech. And now it was time to go. I had a bus to catch.

On the boardwalk we sat down to put on our shoes. We both gazed at the setting sun over the beautiful Mediterranean Sea. Getting Rick's attention I told him about my true feelings for him.

"I hope you still feel the same about me," I added.

To my relief, he broke into a wonderful "Rick" smile and laughed.

"Yes I do! This is the best day ever!" he exclaimed.

Together we walked to the Central Bus Station where he bought me a bag of sunflower seeds, and gave me an affectionate kiss. We had to say good bye, not knowing when we would see each other again.

Relieved, I returned to the hospital, knowing that our relationship had been mended. But even more than that, we both had spoken about our serious intentions to deepen our relationship.

Expecting to hear from Rick within the week, I began to get worried when three weeks had passed and I still had not heard from him. *What happened?* I wondered. *Did he have second thoughts?*

Scheduled to have a long weekend off from work, I decided to go home to my parents, it was there that I learned why Rick had not phoned - Israel was at war! I knew there were disturbances and unrest on the Lebanese border, but again my nursing life blocked out everything else. I had been unaware of the political events taking place. Never in my life would I have dreamed that my Rick would be called up to fight. Because his unit had been going on maneuvers for the last couple of months, Rick had often traveled north, this had been the reason he could stop and visit me at the hospital. At that time he was under strict orders not to tell anyone what his unit was doing at the northern border, and I now found out that they had crossed into Lebanon!

The atmosphere in the hospital grew serious, I could feel the tension mounting every day. Because the Poriah hospital served a limited region, we knew that we probably would not be receiving seriously wounded soldiers. Still, we had to be on call. Every hour we watched and listened to the news, and regularly we heard helicopters flying the wounded soldiers to the larger hospitals of Afula and Haifa.
As often as I could, I met with other believers in the area where we shared information and prayed for the situation.

CHAPTER 19

"... and I will go anywhere with you!"

Weeks later, I was at my parent's home again when Rick phoned! Hearing his voice was so wonderful, so exciting!

"I've gotten leave from the front and I'm on my way back to the kibbutz," he said. "My convoy will stop in Afula, so I'll ask my officer if he can drop me off in the town center."

While my dad left to pick Rick up, Mom and I quickly began to prepare some food as we figured Rick would be hungry. Finally Rick walked through the front door! It was so amazing to see him! I couldn't take my eyes off of him. Happy and proud, I thanked God for his safety. After more than four weeks of fighting in Lebanon, Rick looked like a wild man. During his army time he developed a lot of muscles, but now he also had a rugged look. His long, unkempt hair and beard were covered with white dust. His uniform looked as if he had not taken it off for many days. His face was lined, he obviously was tired, but to me he was stunning, so terribly handsome.

We invited him to eat and tried to be sensitive to his emotional needs, for we didn't know yet what he had seen or taken part in. At first Rick could not eat; he excused himself and sat for a while on the porch by himself, then asked if he could take a shower. Dressed in clean clothes my father had given him, Rick became more relaxed. My dear parents made themselves scarce, giving us the opportunity to be alone. Sitting together on the porch looking at the stars, I wished he would never have to leave me again.

Because I still had two days off, I decided to go with Rick to his kibbutz, Ramat Hakovesh, which I loved. It was wonderful traveling together again, and we both felt a spirit of independence. Even riding the buses or hitch-hiking, a common way of traveling then, was liberating. This was our time together, and we were alive. For this short period of time we were both out of uniform and, thus, free from obligations, so we decided to make the best of it.

Rick was welcomed enthusiastically by his kibbutz family with hugs and smiles. Motti and Ruti, who had been privy to many of Rick's stories and escapades, had been anxiously following the news about the war. The short walk to the communal dining room took much longer than usual as everyone wanted to hear Rick's story or tell their own.

Soon, most of the kibbutzniks knew that "Rick and Dafna are together". We visited friends and talked for hours in his room. When I spent the night on the kibbutz Rick gave me his room and he went to Moti and Ruti's. I respected Rick's strong convictions about keeping our relationship pure, which also was a strong witness to those around us.

The next time Rick came home while on leave, he proposed to me, and this time there was no hesitation from my part, no consideration about my job or duties. However, my answer was the same,

"Rick, you are my best friend ever and I will go anywhere with you."

Together, we literally have gone to many different places, always following the Lord's lead. We have raised two wonderful boys, Daniel and Yohai. And we are still each other's best friends.

CHAPTER 20

Wedding, Honeymoon
and Life on the Kibbutz

Dafna and I married in February, 1983, and the kibbutz gave us a
four-month honeymoon.

Because my mother had not been able to come to the wedding, we
flew to Toronto where she threw us a big party. We also visited
Dafna's relatives in the USA and enjoyed a long honeymoon with a
grand finale at Taos where we went skiing.

Travelling through Colorado, we visited Dafna's Uncle Max and Aunt
Judy who had been missionaries in New Guinea. They built a cabin in
Colorado that was similar to the primitive cabins they had been used
to while on the mission field. Dafna recognized the cabin from her
childhood and noticed her uncle had built another one – a two story
cabin. Upstairs were the living quarters and downstairs a huge open
area for church or ministry purposes, like alcohol rehabilitation, while
he lived in the other cabin.

Uncle Max had sold the buildings but later had to foreclose the deal because the people didn't pay. The first cabin had been the home of a family who had lived there with their goats and chickens, while the other building had been turned into a barn. We would only years later understand the significance of this little visit in Colorado.

After our honeymoon, we returned to Israel. Dafna first worked in the children's home on the Kibbutz and later at the Kfar Saba hospital; I worked in the banana fields.
Everyone knew I wanted to work full-time in the arts, carving wood, and if the kibbutz had been able to create a branch that rendered income they would have let me. Even though this was not possible, they gave me a small shed that was turned into a studio and also sent me to a three-month art class in Tel Aviv. But even the "Kibbutz artist", like everybody else, had to do his full share of the work.
We felt at home amongst our kibbutz friends who accepted both of us completely.

CHAPTER 21

Spreading our Wings

About one and a half years into our marriage, when Dafna was in the process of becoming a kibbutz member, the Lord clearly began to speak to us about going into the arts full-time.

We realized that by staying on the kibbutz, art would become a hobby. Our future children would be kibbutzniks, raised in the children's home. We wanted to raise them according to our faith, with their parents. Dafna and I both knew that the time had come to leave the "protected" life we so much enjoyed and take a plunge into the deep unknown outside the kibbutz.

It was very hard to leave our friends and "family" as we knew each and every one on the kibbutz. We also faced many practical challenges: we had to rent our own apartment, buy furniture, open a bank account, and Dafna had to cook our meals. We were exchanging a rural setting for a two-bedroom apartment in Kfar Yona, near Netanya. Ruth and Yatzuk, Israeli friends, also lived in that village. While Dafna continued to work in the Kfar Saba hospital, I was a gardener for the USA embassy families who lived in Kfar Shmariyahu. Each day I rode my ten-speed bike to work. It was a 70 kilometers ride, but worth it, for they paid me cash, in dollars. During this time of hyper inflation one dollar was about 1,000 lira. On Shabbat we went to a house meeting in Netanya.

Even though one of our bedrooms had been turned into a studio, I didn't use it much because I was working full-time as a gardener. Only after work was there time for artistic creativity.

I knew that I needed more training in sculpting. What I needed was basic knowledge, such as how to sharpen chisels and what kind of chisels to use.

"Do you think I should go to art school?" I asked my friend Benjamin.

"There is a lot of 'weirdness' going on in art schools," Benjamin warned me, "but if you're thinking about going to one, really check it out and ask the Lord before you decide. Don't take it for granted that you have to go to art school."

CHAPTER 22

Visiting the Grandparents in Toronto

When our first son Daniel was born in 1985, of course my parents wanted to see their grandson. They learned that it was cheaper to send us money for tickets and spend about six months in Canada than for them to come to Israel and stay in a hotel. Together with our two-month old baby, we made a stopover in Italy where we studied the works of Michelangelo. I had read his life story and seen the movie, but now we feasted our eyes on his main works in Florence and Rome.

While we stayed with my parents in Toronto, I inquired at the local art school where my aunt also studied. I asked around and met a few teachers, told them that I wanted to sculpt and that I only needed technical information. They told me that in order to get an art degree, I had to learn painting, silk painting and all kinds of other stuff I didn't want or need. Sitting in on one of the classes, I saw what they were teaching the students. Sensing the atmosphere, I remembered Benjamin's words and knew he was right – there was a lot of "weirdness" going on there. There was also the financial aspect of this school. I now was a married man with a small child, and by the time I would have my art degree, after four years of study, we would be about $ 25,000 in debt, that is, IF I also worked on the side. *If you get into debt, you will never return to Israel!* the Lord kept warning me. The answer was clear cut - no art school.

In order to support ourselves during our time in Canada, I had been working as a bus, truck and taxi driver (a redeemed taxi driver) and had earned enough money to pay for another six months of living expenses. "Wheeltrans", a Toronto taxi service for the handicapped and elderly, had been a good job that offered many benefits, including health insurance.

My family thought that I would never leave such a secure job and would buy a house and stay in Toronto. Dafna and I knew that our time in Canada would be temporary and that eventually we would return to Israel. We began visiting sculpture shows in Toronto, and especially the wood art exhibitions. We came across stunning pieces of art from Joe Dampf that we particularly liked and learned that he happened to live in Toronto.

"Hello, you don't know me," I told Joe over the phone, "but I've seen your work and I really like it. I'm like a baby sculptor and don't really know anything. Is there a possibility of getting together? Have a cup of coffee and just talk a little about your work? "

"Are you from Toronto?" Joe wanted to know.

"No, I'm from Israel."

Joe became very interested. He wanted to know more about Israel and the kibbutz.

"I definitely want to meet you!" he said.

After we met for coffee, Joe took me to his house and showed me the whole process, from idea to finished product.

"I'm teaching night school class," Joe said. "You're invited to come to this class, but besides that, we can always meet in between when I have time."

Joe and I really connected and I could ask him any question I wanted, either on the phone, during coffee or in art class. Not only did I ask lots of questions, I also needed hands-on experience, some kind of apprenticeship. When Joe taught me how to work the clay, the first piece I did was a portrait of my father that I carved and then fired. At first, I didn't like the messy material and the feeling of clay, because I was so used to working with the hard wood.

During the ten months we were in Toronto, Joe and I met regularly. He taught me how to make a mold, cast it in plaster and how to use the same pointing system that Michelangelo used to transfer the information from the model to the stone. Having tidbits of knowledge about this way of working, I hadn't known how to implement the technique, until Joe showed me. By this time I knew that I had learned a lot, and the time had come to learn to fly by myself. But how? And where?

CHAPTER 23

From Lake Cottage to Colorado Cabin

My parents owned a small lake cottage up in northern Ontario, and we asked my father if we could stay there for a while. The time had come to find out if the life of a full-time artist was for me or not. Until then I had been sculpting here and there, for short periods of time, with a job on the side, but never had I been able to work for days on end. *Will I run out of ideas?* I wondered. *Will it become boring? Will we run out of money?* This was going to tell us if my life as an artist was really from the Lord or from my own desire.

It was early spring when we moved into the cottage, and the boat house became my studio. During this time the ice began to melt; we planned to stay there until late fall, just before winter would set in again.

The moment I began working in my studio near the lake, the ideas began to flow. They kept coming, and I soon established a steady work rhythm. However, I no longer was single with a lot of free time on my hands, but a husband and a father of a small son.
The distance between the cottage and the studio was too far to shout; therefore, Dafna announced lunchtime by blowing a small moose horn. To be in the middle of an art project and then suddenly hear the sound telling me lunch was ready always gave me a feeling of wonder.

Walking up to the house, seeing my beloved wife and son, I stepped into a different world – a world of order. It was such a difference from the studio I had just left – there was chaos, woodchips everywhere and all those partially finished pieces. Stepping from my creative world into the orderly home helped me to keep my sanity - extremely important for an artist. Consistency within the home fuels the creative juices, and the link with normal life creates a much needed balance.

Over the years I've met many artists who have crashed and are burnt-out because they lacked this balance. Often they are (multiple times) divorcees or living together with someone. Most of the (unbelieving) artists have unstable relationships and cannot handle the "normal" world. Unable to find relief in their chaotic world, they abuse drugs or alcohol to escape the mass disorder in their lives.

How blessed I was to have Dafna, a busy young mother with whom I could have interesting conversations during lunch until I returned to the studio. Daniel loved to stand on the porch and shout at the top of his voice. He didn't bother anybody, because we were totally alone up there.

The six months passed quickly and the six finished art pieces proved that I could work as a full-time artist. It was a wonderful feeling! But what to do next? Where to live during the winter?
"What about your uncle's cabin in Colorado?" I asked Dafna.
"I think he's trying to sell it," Dafna said.

A phone-call to Uncle Max told me that he was still trying to sell these two cabins. While I tried to work out the terms, Dafna struggled with the idea of moving there. She knew it would be hard to live in that area. For about five days she prayed and thought about this move and then told the Lord, "If this is Your will, then I'll do it."
It turned out to be His will and it was time to pack and move to Colorado!

While I went back to work in order to have the finances to move to Colorado, Dafna and Daniel stayed with her brother's family in Colorado Springs until I drove down with the trailer and our belongings. Cleaning and renovating was a major undertaking, because the two story cabin had not been lived in for a few years. A demolition company provided us with cheap material needed to refurbish the upstairs that was to be our living quarters. Downstairs was turned into a workshop. A rural road led into the small town with shops and a library. Thankfully, we also made a few friends there.

In Colorado we bumped into a foundry for bronze. As usual, I began to ask them all kinds of questions. Their reaction surprised me.

"Who are you?" They eyed me suspiciously. "We don't know you."

I soon discovered that foundry men did not have the time nor the patience to deal with beginning artists.

Working with bronze was my desire, but I needed someone who wasn't put off by my questions and who was willing to show me how to go about working with this precious material. I kept praying that one day the Lord would lead me to the right man.

In the Colorado Mountains

CHAPTER 24

Learning to Trust and Obey

Colorado and Toronto had been a good learning process but it was time to head back to Israel. Daniel was about four years old now, so we rented a nice apartment that had room for us as a bigger family and also had a studio. The Lord began to speak about this next period of time" "It will be do or die," He told me, "Dafna must not work as a nurse, and you are not to make your needs known to anyone!" These would be the conditions.

Trying to keep our part of the bargain, Dafna and I lived as frugally as possible without starving. We didn't own a car, so I rode my 10 speed bike everywhere.
Learning to live by faith was a gradual process and most people don't believe someone can work full-time in the arts and actually live, so this definitely would be a challenge. It seemed that each time our bank account was down to almost zero, we either sold a piece of art or received money for a commission. Knowing the average monthly amount we needed to live helped us to calculate how many extra months a big commission would give us plus some extra breathing space.

Around the time our bank account was zero, Julie, a friend from Colorado, came to visit us. She had bought a piece of sculpture and still owed us $300. Knowing that certain bills were due, Dafna and I were getting a little nervous about how to pay them, but told each other, "Well, the Lord brought us to the last minute, but Julie's coming! She owes us that $ 300!"
In those days, not only would such an amount pay for all our bills, but it would also give us a breather for a few weeks.

Borrowing the "community" van from the fellowship, I picked Julie up from Netanya's central bus station. She blessed us with a bag of goodies like toothpaste and special treats from the States.

We had lunch together and enjoyed each other's company, but all the time I wondered, *Lord, should I remind her about the $300? Should I bring it up?* And each time I strongly felt, *Don't say one word!* This was so very hard for me. *Lord,* I pleaded, *I'm not ASKING for money from Julie, but Julie OWES us this 'huge' sum we so desperately need right now!*

Even though I did my best to enjoy the visit my mind constantly circled back to the question, *Is she going to give us the money or not?* When it was time to drive Julie back to the central bus station, I was almost beside myself. *Lord, enough already!* I inwardly groaned. *I haven't said anything to Julie. Come on! She's leaving!* It was time to say good-bye. While I stayed in the van, Dafna walked Julie to the right platform. By then, I sort of accepted the fact she hadn't given us the money, but on the other hand hoped she would slip the $300 (and maybe even more) at the last moment into Dafna's hand and it would be all over.

When Dafna returned to the van, I made a huge effort to sound controlled. "Well? Did she give you some money?"

"No. She didn't!" Dafna said. "She didn't even bring it up!"

"Wow! What's going on, Lord?" I exclaimed.

Looking at each other, we both thought, *O.K. this is really hard, Lord!* So we then prayed, trying not to be bewildered but not managing very well.

At home, we talked about the financial challenge and tried to encourage each other. By the time we went to bed, we had no idea how this difficult situation was going to be solved.

The very next day, which seemed to be just another normal day, there was a letter in the mail from a church in North Carolina. Art Carlson, an old friend of ours, pastored a church there, but we had not seen or been in touch with him for at least six to seven months.

When we opened the envelope from Grace Church, inside was a check made out to both of us for $300. There was no note, no letter, only the check for the exact amount of money that Julie had owed us. I wrote Art a letter asking him why he had sent us the money.

A few weeks later, the reply came, "I just had this idea from the Lord that I needed to send you that amount of money."

The miraculous way the Lord provided for our needs became a foundation stone for us. By this lesson with Julie, we understood that the Lord wanted us to hold on to the principles he showed us. The fact that we wouldn't have to worry about where the money would come from gave us a sense of freedom to make decisions based on trust and not always based on finances.

This principle would later give me the opportunity to work as a foundry apprentice for a year for no pay, knowing the Lord would provide all our needs. Within that year I learned the whole process of casting bronze from beginning to end, and the Lord provided.

While learning to walk in obedience in the area of finances, we noticed that this sometimes created tension with other believers. Some didn't like the fact that Lord had made it clear to us that we were not to make our needs known.

"You have a very arrogant attitude," one believer told me. "You must make your needs known in order for people to give. You're not humble enough, that's it."

"If the Lord tells you to send out letters asking for support, fine," I often told people. "But don't judge others who are led to act differently."

When I was still a young believer, I read books about Hudson Taylor and Muller. The one about Reese Howels I've read over twenty times. These wonderful books taught me how these great men of God trusted Him to supply the needs for their God-given ministries.

Also my friends Benjamin and Art Carlson taught me a lot about the importance of a right relationship to money in the Kingdom of God.

CHAPTER 25

The Foundry Apprentice

Eventually, after getting back to Israel we caught up with our friend Yatzuk from Kfar Yona. When I told him about my disappointing encounter with the bronze foundry in Colorado, he said, "My best friend has a foundry in his backyard."

"You never told me you had such a friend" I exclaimed. "Oh! I'd like to meet him!"

Dani Jakobi and I immediately had a great rapport.

"Can you show me everything I need to know about bronze?" I asked him. "Will you teach me?"

When Dani needed help in the foundry but couldn't afford to pay a salary, I offered to help him for a year for free. During the about one and a half years that I worked with Dani, I learned to make molds and waxes and to pour bronze. Because I worked there without a salary, Dani let me cast my first bronze pieces for free. By making smaller pieces, I learned the bronze process along with the creative side of it. But most important of all, throughout that time the Lord reinforced His lesson about finances. From a creative point of view, one of the biggest things I learned during this period was that I didn't have to worry if a piece would sell or not or if it was marketable or not. All I had to do was respond to what I felt the Lord showing me to make and let Him take care of the rest.

Yohai, our second son was born in 1990. Daniel had reached kindergarten age, but we didn't want to send him to a public *gan* (kindergarten) in Netanya. When we heard there was a good school near Tiberias, we asked Dafna's parents if we could rent their apartment in Afula, as they were in the USA. They didn't mind, and we only had to pay minimal rent for the flat in Givat haMoreh.

By that time we had a small car, so every morning I took Daniel to a certain junction to catch the bus to school, went home, worked on a project and was back at 1 p.m. to pick him up again. It wasn't an ideal solution, but it was the best we had during that time.

CHAPTER 26

Return to the Colorado Mountains

In leaving Colorado the first time we had concluded a business arrangement with Dafna's Uncle Max about the cabins. He had owed us some money for doing the renovations but couldn't afford to pay us the cash so he gave us one of the cabins and he kept the cabin that had been cleaned up. We had gone back to Israel without a lot of money but having ownership of one of the cabins.

Just before the outbreak of the Gulf War at the end of 1990, Uncle Max phoned to inform us that he was selling his cabin and that we would have to make a contract of partnership with the new owners. Two weeks later, we flew to Toronto for a visit and from there down to Colorado to close the deal.

The cabin that was ours needed lots of work so we stayed and began to fix it up hoping that at a later stage the couple that had bought Max's would buy ours also. This eventually happened, but again we were in Colorado for almost three more years.

In each time period we learned different aspects of the work. We laid the foundations for sculpting and carving in wood in the kibbutz. Joe Dampf tutored me in Toronto, where I began the process of sculpting in clay and then transferring it into a wood carving. In the cottage in Northern Canada, we established a life-style pattern. During our first time in Colorado I learned stone carving and anatomy and my interest in bronze began. Back in Israel I started to establish working in bronze with Dani. Back in Colorado for the second time, we began to learn how to go out and present the work.

Now we embarked on another adventure. We packed the family into a very old Dodge van with all the work and began visiting churches where we were invited.

Usually the invitation came because we were artists or because we were from Israel or because we were both.

This experience taught us how to display the sculptures and show and sell the work. As time went by, we designed stands and found a good way to pack everything in the van. Often, we had to travel for days to reach the place for the show. I turned the van into a mini-camper: the wooden platform in the back became our bed and behind the driver's seat were two benches facing each other with a table between them. When we finished eating, at 7 p.m., the table went down, mattresses were put on top and the boys were put to sleep. Dafna and I kept on driving until it was time to pull over and for us to go to bed in the back. During this period we also learned how to deal with people, which is an art in itself, especially how to respond when someone showed interest.

Gradually we also began using write-ups that explained what I felt the Lord had been telling me while creating a particular piece of art. This became a very strong and crucial part of presenting our work. During this time I began to make molds using the process which I had learned from Dani. My first reproduction pieces were sold at art shows. From Colorado we made quite a lot of trips with the van to Vancouver, Canada, and many to North Carolina. At Grace Church we established special relationships with the people and the pastor, Art Carlson.

Even though a small bronze figure could sell for about $ 2,000, we knew that most of the people coming to our shows would never be able to afford those prices. $ 200 they might be able to afford. So after a lot of experimenting, we developed a method by which we used the same bronze mold to create a high quality, but affordable, piece of cast stone art.

In the mountain cabin in Colorado, we always lived on what we had. Even though the Lord often kept us at a "0" bank balance, we always had enough for what we needed. Thankfully, I had no problem selling my artwork. Gradually, we began to see a pattern: I would sell a piece of work, receive more money than we needed, and then unexpected

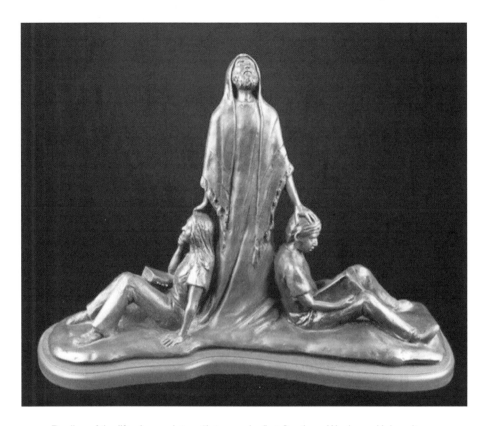

Replica of the life-size sculpture "Intercession" at Southern Wesleyan University Central, South Carolina, USA. Jesus is in the centre; The male student on the right represents education through theory; the female student represents learning through experience. All education is man's vanity without leaning or depending on Jesus and His intercession for each of us.

expenses occurred for which we needed that extra money.
We were now selling work but the Lord would still like to show us His provision. Our bank account would get to zero which would increase our prayers towards the Lord. One day, we planned to visit Dafna's older brother who lived in Colorado Springs, a two hour drive from where we lived. We figured there was enough gas in the tank to get there, but no money to buy gas for the way back. This had become a "gas principle" in our life on the road. If we felt like the Lord was telling us to go somewhere with the work and we had enough gas to get there we would trust him for the gas to get back, so we headed for the Springs.

We left the house a bit stressed and nervous, wondering where we would get the money. Even though the Lord had provided so many times, even at the last moment, we still got nervous. Our mailbox was two miles from the house on the county road, so we stopped to check if we had any mail. To our amazement, inside was a letter with a check for $ 1,500 from a person in New Orleans! Not knowing who this lady was, we read the accompanying letter.

> "*A few weeks ago I was at a ladies meeting attached to my church. I met a woman who had been to Israel over a year ago and taken some photos of your sculptures. She happened to have them and showed me. They made such an impression on me I had to buy two. Please except this check as a down payment.*"

Dafna and I were amazed, only a few minutes before we had been searching for small change to pay for gas, but had decided to trust the Lord and now we were holding a check for $1500. This woman had done some thorough detective work in tracking down our address in Colorado. And that check, sent by a total stranger, found its way to our out-of-the-way address at the exact moment in time we needed it!

The couple that had bought Max's cabin was now interested in ours. We knew it was time to head back to Israel. Colorado was coming to an end. We had learned a lot but now it was time to head home. But where would we live in the country?

This decision became a major turning point that would completely effect the rest of our lives.

Dafna's parents during the time we had been in Colorado had moved to a settlement in Northern Samaria. Settlements had always been a divisive issue in Israel. The settlement movement seemed to attract extreme personalities, which in a way described Joe and Sarah, Dafna's mom and dad.

"Dangerous!" Dafna and I said when we heard about their "pioneering" plans. We thought it was crazy but we were focusing on packing and getting ready to go. We just told ourselves, "The Lord will show us where we will live when we get there."

On arriving home in Israel Dafna's parents collected us at the airport and took us to their house at Cadim.

"Why don't you rent something in Cadim?" Dafna's parents suggested. "Rents are cheap here, and this way you'll have time to look around for a more permanent place in the country to live."

I had been thinking about living in Jerusalem or Tiberias, and this would give us some time to search. We decided that Cadim might be a good place to stay - for a little while.

CHAPTER 27

Intercession in Samaria

Cadim was five hundred meters from Jenin, a Palestinian city of fifty thousand in northern Samaria; the settlement was created to have a Jewish presence in the area. Called the "occupied territories" by some, the West Bank by others, this Biblical heartland was, and continues to be, a controversial part of Israel. Perched high on a hill at the southern end of the Jezreel Valley, Cadim had about a hundred and twenty people. The government's idea behind the settlements was to create a definite Jewish presence when the small villages eventually grew into large towns.
Even though we thought Dafna's parents were crazy to move there, my in-laws didn't perceive this step as abnormal and were accepted by the settlement.

Before returning to Israel, I asked the Lord for the first place that we would come to, to be the place that we could stay. But as our two boys had not seen their grandparents for a long time, we decided to go straight to Cadim. It would just be for a short time, and at least the rent would be reasonable. We decided to stay there while looking for a "real" place to live. Having always rented our homes, and knowing that moving was a big hassle, we would never have considered Cadim, let alone stay there long. Besides, living on a settlement carried a stigma because the "settlers" were perceived to be right-wing, pistol-wheeling, obnoxious people. I didn't want to be identified with them.

Being believers in Jesus, trying to communicate Him through the arts in a country that found it hard to understand who He was, was already controversial enough.
    "Let's stay in Cadim for a few months until we find the right place to live," we decided.

A period of house-hunting began. Looking at several apartments in Jerusalem, nothing felt right. Then I tried other areas, but never had the sense that it was the right place. In the meantime our boys were starting to make friends with some of the kids on the settlement. Dafna's older brother, on a work consignment, also lived there with his family, so for the boys it would be nice to have their cousins nearby. Because things were taking a little longer than expected, we decided to enroll them in school.

Still I resisted being there, despite the facts that Dafna also had good contact with the Cadim women and that we were beginning to get used to living there.

One of the bedrooms of the small house became my workroom. In there, we created the stained glass windows that are now in Christ Church, Jerusalem. While we were living in Kfar Yona and while I was working as a gardener, I met a stained glass artist who taught me how to work with the material. The small bedroom-turned-studio then became the glass workroom. I also taught Dafna, and from then on I made the design while she cut the glass pieces. However, stained glass always had been something I did on the side and something I never actively pursued.

One day I walked over to my in-laws. During the ten minute walk from one end of the settlement to the other side, I passed by an empty house. Having been built by the settlement, it was in the last stages of being sold to a young Israeli couple. *You are to buy this house*, the Lord told me as I passed. The straightforward, abrupt thought or sense seemed to have come from nowhere. Strongly opposed to this idea, I brushed it off and walked on.

But the words kept coming back to me, *I want you to buy this house!* Not liking it at all, I tried to ignore it. However, as a follower of Jesus I had to receive a confirmation whether this was from God or not. After sharing what happened with Dafna, we prayed and I began to fast and seek the Lord about what we should do. Buying a house would have a lot of consequences.

First, this would mean we would become members of Cadim; secondly, it would not be a real investment because of the limited possibilities of potential buyers, in case we wanted to sell again. We had never bought a house before, and I knew for sure that I didn't want to live on the settlement. Even though these were good reasons, the nagging thought persisted.

From experience I knew that sometimes I could be sure an idea was the Lord's will when mine was so very much against it. In this case I knew that it had not been my own idea, so it was possible that it came from God.

"I will do whatever You tell me to do, Lord, but I have to be sure this is from You," I promised.

Dafna and I continued to pray and fast, and, like Gideon, we put out different fleeces. While we agonized over the decision, God kept showing us that this was what He expected us to do: Buy the house!

But what about this other couple who were in the last stages of buying the house? God took care of this problem, for totally unexpected by anyone involved, this couple dropped out and no one heard from them anymore. The house was on the market again. Of course, the settlement members were surprised by this turn of events, but for us it was another confirmation that we were to buy the house.

Despite all this, we still were not completely sure this idea of purchasing a house was from the Lord, so we decided to tell the secretary of the settlement we were believers in Jesus. Even though this administrator knew that we were not Jewish, I wanted him to know about our faith; so if we decided to live on the settlement, nobody could later say we didn't tell them. Secretly I hoped he would be enraged to learn we were believers and perhaps tell us that we had to leave or that we could only rent a house, but not permanently live there. That would suit me fine.

"You can believe whatever you want," he responded. "We want you here."

I was stunned.

Cadim in Samaria (Shomron)

Dafna, however, was quite content to live on the settlement; she didn't mind that we were staying. After having lived in Cadim for over a year she didn't want the boys having to go through another move.

"Why do You want us to stay here, Lord?" I prayed.

This is intercession, I felt Him answer. It was a word I didn't fully understand. Friends of ours called themselves intercessors and some even printed it on their business cards. They told me of the hours and hours of prayer they had been doing for certain issues or subjects, but I couldn't see myself doing that. *Your obedience to Me will be an act of intercession,* I felt the Lord say.

That was something I could do. I knew I could obey, what would come as a result of this obedience would be in the Lord's hands.

Through the years I have come to understand that INTERCESSION is a prayer that is on the heart of the Lord. When we respond to His heart and we obey, His desires will be expressed on this earth. For me that expression and communication would be done through sculpture.

Now we faced another challenge, a big one, for concerning finances the Lord had made it quite clear to us we were not to accumulate debts. Over the years we had been careful not to do so and it had become part of our lives.

"But Lord, when we're going to buy this house, we have to take a mortgage and will be in debt," I told the Lord. "How can this be Your will?" *If you are in debt in obedience to Me, you will only be in debt to Me,* the Lord answered.

Now I was really disturbed. With my whole heart I wanted to do God's will; this was my life. After struggling for days, I happened to read the story of Jesus in the Garden of Gethsemane. In a way I could identify with the heavy feeling the Biblical story described.

When I read, "If it be Your will, take this cup away from me, but Father, Your will be done, not mine", I began to cry and felt the weight of those words.

By then I also realized that it wasn't just me being stubborn, trying to

have my own way, but there would be a price to pay for my obedience. *Am I ready for this?* I wondered and knew that all of us, Dafna and my children also, would be asked to pay a heavy price. All I could do was to trust and follow Him.

In the years that followed, we built our studio for sculpting and working with stained glass. We got to know each and everyone in the settlement, each member with their different personalities. Collectively and individually, we all learned to deal with the dangers living in Shomron entailed.

Both children, nine-year-old Daniel and five-year-old Yohai went by bus to the regional school. It is quite an experience having to accompany your children to the bus stop, watch them board a bulletproof bus which is escorted by an armed soldier, followed by an armed jeep with soldiers. Daily we realized the cost of living in Cadim, but somehow were getting used to the danger surrounding us. As the years went by, it never became normal to be shot at, bombed or attacked by our Arab neighbors while driving to and from the settlement. However, it was always a part of life's possibilities.

After going through that intense struggle and finally agreeing to do God's will, we knew we could trust Him.
Knowing that He was responsible for what happened to us gave us a deep sense of peace.

Despite the fence and the presence of tanks, we felt safe in Cadim

Industrial area at Cadim where I had my studio

CHAPTER 28

The Haifa Conference

We had been living in Cadim for about five years when I travelled to Haifa with two friends to attend a two-day men's conference whose main focus was on prayer. On the way to Haifa, the three of us were joking and telling stories. The two friends shared a room while I had one for myself. During dinner we met the other participants; the overall the atmosphere was light and jovial. I didn't know the two American men who had organized the conference, but it was great seeing friends I hadn't seen for a long time.

When it was time for the first meeting, it felt strange to walk into a small chapel that was only lit by a few candles. It created a mysterious atmosphere, which was definitely more serious than the mood I was in.

"Please, take a seat." The organizers pointed to the chairs that were placed around the perimeter of the room. In the center stood a small table with the elements for communion, bread and wine, lit by a number of candles – it was rather simple.

"Please, prepare yourselves spiritually before partaking," the leader said. "When you feel you are ready, you can come and prayerfully take the elements."

Being a believer for many years, I had taken communion hundreds of times in a lot of different ways and places. This was different, but not entirely so. The room became quiet while everyone examined his own heart before going forward.

My friends and I had been joking so much that I found it hard to become serious, take a good inner look at myself. Somehow I managed to examine my heart, got up to take the wine and the bread. It wasn't in a casual way, but not with deep feelings either.

I thanked the Lord, remembered Him, took the bread and the wine and wanted to return to my chair.

Get down on your knees, I felt the Lord telling me. All over the dimly lit room men were quietly praying by themselves. Even though I thought this was a bit extreme, I obeyed, hoping this act wouldn't draw too much attention to myself. However, the moment I was on my knees the Lord's voice told me, *lie down on your face!*

I didn't like it and struggled against the idea, but decided it would be better to obey and hoped it wouldn't be for too long. Realizing the seriousness of the situation, the moment I was on the floor I began to weep. Softly at first, my weeping grew in intensity. It was as if I was pinned to the floor by a heavy weight. Unable to get up, I sobbed and sobbed. *What's happening, Lord?* I cried inwardly.

By now I was way past feeling embarrassed and realized that God Himself held me to the floor. *What is it, Lord? What do You want?* I prayed. Then all of a sudden I felt Him say, *Would you be willing to give Daniels life for Yakov's salvation?*

Being the settlement administrator, Yakov was a difficult man to deal with. I struggled. *No! I can't. My son for Yakov? I won't! You can't make me, Lord! You can't ask me to do this. Haven't I given enough?* It was so hard. I don't think that there ever has been something as hard as this request. Even though I tried, I couldn't get up from the floor. I felt broken, finished, exhausted. Still weeping for what seemed like a very long time, I continued to wrestle with God's request.

Eventually, I gave up. *Lord, I cannot do it, but I'm willing to be willing, IF You will pull me through.*

The moment I prayed those words, the weight lifted. Despite feeling exhausted, I was at peace, but at the same time wondering what I had done. *What will this mean?* I began to weep again.

Without looking at my friends, I struggled to my feet and left for my room where the battle of emotions and questions continued till exhausted I fell asleep.

I didn't understand what happened, only that I had an encounter with the Lord. What happened to me in that chapel was both scary and intriguing. Certainly, I would never forget this experience and trusted God to make it clear to me when the time came.

Life went on in Cadim.

The sculpting seemed to be our prayer, our intercession. In general, our life had a certain rhythm, but lately there was talk about a possible redeployment. Israel's concessions to the Palestinians for peace would mean we had to leave Cadim.

After living seven years in the settlement, one day I went to the studio as I usually did. It was a beautiful morning. As I walked down the hill towards the industrial area, thinking about the demands of that day, some of the plans and other trivial things, I enjoyed the beautiful view of the Jezreel Valley. Suddenly the Lord interrupted my thoughts with, *The intercession is complete. It is done!*
It had come so out of the blue, so suddenly, that I felt shaken.
What does that mean? I wondered. I had not been sure what the intercession was all about to begin with, so what would its finishing mean? *It all began when we bought the house and joined the settlement, Lord. Does this mean we are now to leave?*
There was no response, only silence.
That particular day I was kept so busy that I didn't have time to think about this encounter.

The next day seemed to start as any normal day. As I walked to the studio, many thoughts floated around in my head.
Now you can pray for the salvation of Israel!
I stopped, thinking, *where did that come from? "Now you can pray for the salvation of Israel"? What does this mean?* I felt shaken. *That's a huge undertaking!* But then I asked the Lord, *Isn't that what I have been doing all these years. This has been the main focus of my prayers, Lord. I had hoped that everything You did somehow worked towards that end.*
Again there was silence, God did not shed any more light on this challenge. I trusted that one day He would show me what it meant.

Over the years I had read a number of books on intercession, but the one which had the biggest impact was *Rees Howells: Intercessor* which showed me "acts" of intercession, ones with a definite beginning and an end, that were completed.

Those that were mentioned began with an act of obedience, a response that was often difficult. Something had to die in the character of the person involved, something he was or desired, and sometimes personal plans had to be sacrificed in obedience to the Lord's call for intercession.

Dafna and I had begun to see a pattern in our lives in relation to working in the arts, particularly the sculpting. Often it seemed the Lord unexpectedly created what we called a "suddenly" which prompted us to search His heart. Most of the time this led us to create a sculpture that in some way reflected that specific word or communication. The creative process was our intercession, while the finished piece was a prophetic word, in the sense that we hoped the sculpture communicated God's heart and word.

With this in mind, I knew the Lord would clarify what He meant and went back to my daily work.

Nothing more seemed to happen.

CHAPTER 29

The 'Payback' Word

We had been friends with Graham Cooke for a number of years when in the year 2001 he invited me to attend a conference in Southampton where he was scheduled to speak. Graham had bought a large number of our small sculptures and had often invited me to conferences in his home church in England. This time, however, I was so swamped with work that I couldn't think about going. After casually praying about it, one morning the Lord told me, *GO!* I resisted, but the more I balked, the more spiritual pressure I experienced. Eventually I gave in and began making preparations to fly to England.

"Payback" – what a strange name for a conference, I thought. *And the timing, right when we are celebrating Purim in Israel.*
This is the holiday about the story of Esther and the salvation of the Jews. I knew Graham had not intentionally connected the conference to this holiday but thought it to be interesting.
Upon arriving in Southampton on the first day of the conference, I was surprised and moved to see that Graham displayed all the art pieces he had bought from us over the years. "I hope this will bring in some more orders for you," he told me.

That Thursday evening the main focus was on worship. Knowing the worship band fairly well, I looked forward to the evening.
That evening when worship began, the music seemed to envelop me. I was surprised it went intense and deep very fast.
Looking at the band, I noticed a woman playing the violin whom I never had seen before. The music was loud and I thought, *nice that there is a violin but who would hear it?* This was just a small moment of distraction that was carried away with the music. I closed my eyes and let myself drift in the worship. I enjoyed this sense of being in the presence of the Lord, experiencing this peace, this place of quiet inside myself.

Suddenly the music stopped. Graham took the mike and said,

"This is the year of "Pay Back", this is the year of unprecedented grace and favor, this is the year that the Lord is going to pay back all that has been ravaged against you; everything that the enemy has taken from you, all that the locusts have stolen from you will be returned."

He spoke those strong words with authority to the three to four hundred people that were in the hall that night. *There must be some people here who had an abusive past,* I thought, *and the Lord is going to heal these wounds. Good word, but not for me.*

The band resumed playing, so I sat back to enjoy the music, but the atmosphere had somehow shifted.

The second day of the conference Graham invited me up front to say a few words. I think he wanted people to see that I was the artist who had made the sculptures, in case someone wanted to place an order. That evening the session began with another burst of music, and again I found myself drifting into a place with the Lord; His almost tangible presence made me alert. As the music soared, again Graham took the mike and repeated the same words he had spoken yesterday,

"This is the year of 'Pay Back'; this is the year of unprecedented grace and favor...."

I became irritated, for I was enjoying the worship which he again had interrupted. *Graham, all the same people are here,* I thought selfishly. *You've said this same thing last night. Why repeat it?*

I detached myself from listening until Graham shifted, he changed something that pulled my attention back to the words.

"This is not for you personally, but this is for the people that I have attached you to!"

I will never be able to fully explain this, but the moment Graham said, "this is for the people that I have attached you to!" I suddenly felt like the Lord was speaking directly to me. Without any warning I suddenly felt like I couldn't breath, like I had been punched in the stomach; I felt like all the air in the room was sucked out, and I burst into tears.

Unable to stand, I sat bent over in the chair and cried uncontrollably. In this moment of struggling I cried out to the Lord, "What is this? What is going on?"

I felt the Lord speak, *Pay Back for the Jewish people is six million!* My mind still whirling, I didn't understand, but because of the number I figured that it had something to do with the Holocaust.

The Holocaust? I don't get it. Lord, I don't understand what is happening to me right now, but why the Holocaust?

I felt the Lord speak again, *I am going to bring into the Kingdom six million for what was ravaged against them in the Holocaust.*

This jerked me, I didn't understand what had been communicated to me, what had happened to me. However, I knew it was Him.

Slowly I came back to myself. My head was full of questions and no answers. Knowing for sure that this was from God, it scared me like crazy. The music had been playing again for some time but it seemed distant. Trying to get some rest, I had no clue what He meant or how the Lord would do what he had said. Six million! Those numbers were too big for me; I couldn't grasp it.

Beginning to feel calmer, I thought, *What do You want from me, through this word? I can't relate to this, can't grasp it.*

Unable to deny this was the Lord, I had to put it on some kind of inner shelf to be examined later. Right now, I needed to rest and make an effort to pull myself together again. During the remainder of the night I kept wondering why Graham's last words had triggered such a powerful reaction within me. It had deeply touched the almost twenty-five year relationship I had with both the Jewish people and their land.

The Holocaust and the birth of Israel had been with me from the beginning of my walk with the Lord. Even before I had given my life to the Lord, those two subjects had triggered tears. Tonight, the Lord had touched this foundation, as if He wanted to build on it. But what? I didn't want to think about it. The Holocaust was a place you only went to with questions for which you would never receive answers. It would be far better to stay clear of it and not go there at all.

Is this the beginning of a new sculpture? I wondered.

Similar situations had been used by the Lord to get my attention, and in response I had done some sculptures, but the prompting had never been as strong as it was now. It seemed holy, untouchable, and I needed some distance. *You'll have to explain some more,* I told the Lord, but wasn't sure I could take it if He revealed this "more". *Do I really want this confirmation?*

That night I fell asleep with my question, but slept well. The next day was filled with the activities of the conference but I was not really there. My thoughts carried me to the world of questions, 'Pay Back', six million, the kingdom? I felt all right but disconnected and didn't want to talk to anyone but to be left alone with my wonderings.
At the lunch break, while hoping to find a quiet place outside to eat by myself, the violinist ambushed me in the foyer. She caught me just as I was trying to leave. "Are you the sculptor from Israel that spoke a few words yesterday?" she asked.
When I reluctantly answered yes, she told me she wanted to ask me some questions. "Would you like to join me for some coffee?"
Even though I wanted to say "no", I somehow found myself agreeing to come.

Ruth Fazal was a professional violinist who lived and worked in Toronto. She began by telling a story of how the Lord had pulled her into a creative process of writing an oratorio. I didn't know what an oratorio was but knew that it was something musical and figured that I would learn more as I listened. When Ruth explained that this piece of music was based on the poetry of Jewish children from the Holocaust she had my full attention. I became fascinated with her story on how her creative process through music had touched this place of terrible memory.
It fascinated but also scared me that I heard this story now, the morning after I had received this heavy and bewildering word from the Lord. I didn't tell her what had happened to me for I didn't want to speak it out loud, so I just listened.

When Ruth learned that Dafna, the boys and I would be in Toronto to visit my parents, she suggested to meet in Toronto in about three months. At the same time I also had to install a large, bronze sculpture at a university in northern Indiana.

Later it seemed a coincidence that the theme of that piece was Jesus struggling over the cup of sorrows in the garden of Gethsemane. Gradually I would learn the significance of God's timing.

Three months later, when we met in Toronto, again over coffee, Ruth told us how her work on the oratorio proceeded. It was nice getting to know each other a bit more, so we told her about our schedule and plans.

"Dafna and I will be in North Carolina to start on a new piece of sculpture and then return to Israel," I told her.

"And I'll be doing a conference in South Carolina at the same time!" Ruth became excited.

We decided to meet each other again there.

CHAPTER 30

The Seven Last Words

Mid-summer in 2001, it took me four hours to drive to the conference in South Carolina to meet Ruth. As Dafna had not been able to join me, I planned to stay for only one night. The conference was organized by Ruth Fazal and a man named Gary Wiens from Kansas City whom I met later that day together with a few of the musicians.

The next day, during a break between sessions, someone told me I had to stay for another night because Ruth and Gary were going to do the "Seven Last Words" together.
"What is that?" I asked.
"It is a poem based on Jesus' last seven words on the cross," they explained. "Ruth and Gary have performed it at different conferences. The poem is from John's perspective, as he was the only disciple who stayed during the crucifixion."
I decided to stay and drive back late to North Carolina afterwards without having any idea what was in store for me.

Gary's narration of the poem, accompanied by Ruth's melodic violin music, was powerful, full of rising emotions and crushing realities. I sensed John's pain upon seeing and hearing his best friend struggle to speak out those last words while at the same time watching Him suffer on that cross. It evoked so many visual pictures in me that it was as if I was there, with them. Each spoken word, playing out its own drama, was followed by John's response. Spell-bound, I listened to the hour-long recitation.
During coffee afterwards, Gary and Ruth asked me what I thought about the poem.
"I don't have any words for it." No words, only pictures floating through my head, crashing into each other. I had to sort them out.

---

[1] Poem "The Seven Last words of Christ" by Gary Wiens used with permission

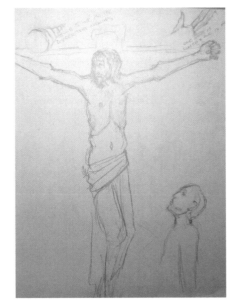

So throughout the four-hour drive back to our place, I made many sketches in my head. I was certain I had to make something of them. A drawing? A sculpture? But how was I to communicate these crucifixion words through one figure?

It was late at night when I got back, but taking my sketchbook, I quickly drew basic stick figures so that, for now at least, I had a visual reminder of what I had seen. Over the next two weeks I continued to spend a lot of time on these drawings which by then had developed into seven crucifixion scenes, and facing each one were seven figures in different body stances relating to each of the words. I struggled to get it right, because even though the crucifixion had to be seen as a whole, at the same time it was divided into seven parts.

One night I sketched seven panels and divided them with pillars of fieldstones. Suddenly I felt the Lord break into my focus in sketching. *What do stones that are piled on top of each other represent?* He asked. This seemed abrupt but I immediately I thought of the people of Israel entering the land after crossing the Jordan and the priests piling stones on top of each other. A **memorial** was the word that came to mind. The moment this thought came I started to experience the emotions of the "Pay Back" word. I wasn't prepared for this, but again the Lord spoke and said, *count how many pillars of stone you have done.* There were six.

Ever since that "Pay Back" word had burst into my life about six to seven months before, the Lord had not revisited it. I sincerely had hoped that it would stay that way but the six fieldstone dividers brought it all back, even the powerful emotion it had evoked in me then. It alarmed me. *A memorial to the six million? That can't be related to the seven last words of the crucifixion! I can't put the crucifixion and the Holocaust together!* Inwardly I almost yelled, shouted: *You can't put them together and expect to live, in Israel!* Most Israeli's would say it was the crucifixion that created the Holocaust. The new revelation of the memorial to six million stayed with me for days, and I didn't know what to do with it.

After committing my life to the Lord, I had told Him that if He would make His will known to me, I was going to respond, I would do what He wanted. At that period in my life it seemed the right thing to say, and I meant what I said. This time, however, I would have to pay a very high price for what the Lord seemed to be asking of me.

I began looking at the seven lasts words, pondering their meanings:
> *"Father forgive them, they don't know what they do"*
> *"Today you will be with me in Paradise"*
> *"Mother this is your son, Son this is your mother"*
> *"My God my God why have you forsaken me"*
> *"I thirst"*
> *"It is finished"*
> and finally *"Into your hands I commend my spirit".*

Each one carried a mystery, a depth. Each would be a door way that called me to enter through.

Feeling then drawn to the disciple John, I wondered how I could represent him. Like a young Jewish man wearing a T-shirt and jeans, a modern version of the disciple? *The memorial to the six million murdered Jews represented by the six pillars will be something between the Lord and me*, I mused, wanting to keep the meaning hidden. By looking at the work, no one would link it to the Holocaust. Satisfied by this solution, I took my sketchbook and began to expand my initial drawings. *Perhaps there should also be water in this,* I thought. *Water flowing over the surface of the crucifixion panels.*

We had been keeping in touch with Ruth, and she knew that I was working on a project that had to do with the poem. During a phone conversation I told her of incorporating the "fountain" idea. Interrupting me she said, "Wait a second!" A few minutes later she was back on the line. "This is a verse the Lord gave me when I began writing the Oratorio. It's from Jeremiah nine." And then she quoted,

> *"Oh Lord, that my head was a spring of water*
> *and my eyes a fountain of tears,*
> *that I might weep day and night*
> *for the slain of my people."*

Deeply touched, I was also stunned, realizing that the idea of adding water to this work was connected to the tears shed over the slain people of Israel. Unknowingly, Ruth had given the work its name. Now I also understood the meaning behind it: it was an intercession for the slain, a remembrance of them. I wanted to keep the Holocaust at a safe distance from the Crucifixion but the Lord was not allowing it.

The time had come to take the next step.

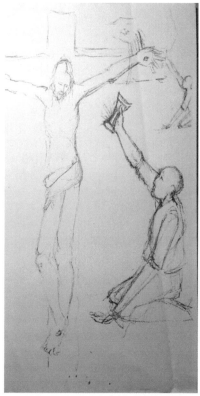

Prologue – Before Your Feet

Before Your feet, o Lamb of God,
I take my place.
I breathe Your Name
As tears in silent eloquence declare my thanks.
Your shattered visage announces healing for this broken image,
Thunders Your passion, avows Your love.....
...
I take Your hand,
For You have stretched it out for me upon the cross.
How could I keep from foll'wing You, Who are my joy, my very Life.
Your precious love has won the day,
And drawn me near.

Epilogue – the Morning

The morning came,
And once again I find myself before Your feet.
Your eyes, alive with fire I've never seen, are fixed on me again,
And I know.
...
I'd turned to go, and there You stood,
And took my hand, and called my name, and drew me near.
Your beating heart against my cheek released the tears,
As once again I took my place the one You live, inside Your heart.
And so the morning came,
and once again I find myself before Your feet.
Your eyes alive with fire I've never seen, are fixed on me again,
And now I know.
I know.

CHAPTER 31

A Heavenly Commission

By now I had received enough confirmations and decided to make six scale models, each one representing John.[1] The scaled model's 12 inch figures (about 30 cm) would stand before a nine foot (about 3 meters) long and two foot (60 cm) high wall of crucifixion panels. For the figure of John, I used pictures that I had taken of a Jewish friend's face, with his consent of course. He had a great face for John, warm, sympathetic with a slightly receding hairline of his otherwise full, curly hair.

To create a sculpture, I always begin by building a wire structure as a skeleton to support the clay. Even a wire armature communicates something through its simple body language, and in this case it gave me the basic direction for the figure as he responded to each of the seven words. After body mass with the clay was added, the figure became more detailed, albeit still basic. Leaving the head bald, I decided to keep the hair for last and steadily worked on the beginning phases of each stance the models would have and their bodily expressions.

I already had a certain idea in mind for the first panel of "Father forgive them, they don't know what they do." Then the moment came to work on the details of the model's hair, the facial expression and the hands. Always when reaching this stage of the sculpture, I feel the seriousness of working on these parts as they express the majority of the communication. One can either break or convey the emotional message. The hands turned out well, the face was developing nicely, and now I came to the usual easy part that gives the figure distinction - the hair. However, the moment I added the hair, it didn't look right, so I took it off by removing the clay.

---

[1] These bronze mini models are now in IHOP, Kansas City

Again I tried adding the hair, which looked all right, but even though the proportions of the face and the head were correct, somehow the hair didn't match the face. So I took it off again, and again, and then stopped. Throughout the years, while modeling hundreds of figures, at one point or another I always struggled to get the head and face right. But this time it was different; the hair was causing the problem. Creating a model had never been so hard before.

After my umpteenth, failed attempt I became so frustrated that I decided to leave the figure for what it was and move on to the next panel, "Today you will be with me in Paradise."

There were no problems with the initial sculpting. Even in this basic form I could feel the word that moved me, and I enjoyed working on it. But then, as I reached the stage of adding the hair, I felt strangely blocked. Again I tried to give the figure hair, but couldn't get it right. *Everything else seems right, so what is it with the hair?* I wondered. Deciding to leave it bald also, I moved on to the next figure until all the seven sculptures representing John were ready. But all of them were bald. I didn't understand it, for these clay models all seemed to express what I had felt during the recital of the poem. How could it feel right and wrong at the same time?

Maybe it has to do with something I'm going through, I thought and decided to continue with the next stage – making the molds. That is when I cast the figure in wax, making it ready for the bronze casting part. Because I would still be able to make changes in the sculpture, I decided to leave the problem of the hair for later. But then, when I had to finish the sculpture in order to continue, I was still unable to put the hair on the figures. Utterly frustrated I prayed, "Lord, what is this? I don't get it!"

What was the most visual identification of the men and women in the concentration camps? The Lord seemed to ask me.

Immediately I knew: their heads were shaved! I was brought back to the moment I had received the "payback" word. Even though I didn't want to go there, I was given no choice.

A wave of emotion swept over me and I began to weep. It was as if I felt God's own feelings on this subject.

It was so hard, so heart wrenching. It scared me.
When I continue to work on this project I won't have a place to hide!
I knew. *If this John model becomes a person from a concentration camp, not only will his head be shaved but he must be dressed in the striped prison clothes; everyone will immediately know that this is the Holocaust.* But it was the Lord speaking, and I had promised to obey him. I felt miserable.

In a sense, I grieved over this revelation for days because it changed everything I had intended to do. While the focus had been on the poem's seven last words of Jesus and John's response, it now became the response of the Holocaust to the seven last words. *I may lose all my Israeli friends,* I thought, *they all know that I am a believer in Jesus and they respect that, but they will say you have gone too far and would have nothing to do with me anymore.* I found this thought very hard, and it took me a long time to say, "All right, Lord. Your will be done" and obey His prompting.

Suddenly I understood how John must have felt while standing at the feet of Jesus – he and I shared the same Lord. In my own, small way, I could relate to the poem's words that were spoken as a close friend and follower of Jesus. But the Holocaust? How could I know the feelings of the Holocaust? How would a figure representing the Holocaust react to the words spoken from the crucifixion. The crucifixion of Jesus is what the Jews perceive to be the source of hatred towards them.

My final cry to the Lord was, "How do I create a memorial if I myself don't have memory? I am a Gentile; there is no one in my family that is Jewish, no one that has gone through the Holocaust! I have to a have a beginning point, something of memory to draw from within me!"
Pushing further, I added, "I am Canadian, I don't even have a national memory that I could pull from. If I had been born in France or Holland, at least there would be a national memory!"
Thinking about my words, they made sense and I felt justified.
By using this as an argument I could walk away.

In my moment of self satisfaction I felt the Lord break in with three very simple words, *But I do!* He pushed further, *I have a memory of every child, every man, every woman, every cry from every pit, every train car, every gas chamber, you create from My memory not yours!*

Having arrived at my last point of resistance, I embraced His heart.

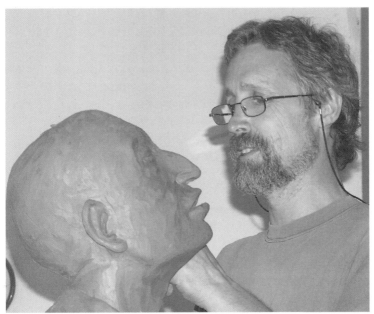

CHAPTER 32

Sculpting and Meditating

In the spring of 2003, many drawings and models later, I began preparations for the seven, full-size, relief panels representing Jesus' seven last phrases which He spoke from the cross. The panels were to be six feet wide by twelve feet high (about two by four meters). My studio on the settlement wasn't big, but I managed to place the seven frames on the floor of my already tightly packed workspace in such a way that I could work and see all of them.

All the while I was sculpting the figure for each particular word, I meditated and thought on it. *How can I express that word through His face while at the same time convey such unimaginable pain?* I wondered. *Does He forget the pain for a moment when He speaks the word, or are they part of each other? Does the pain give strength or authority to the word? In the wall I'm creating, how can I let His hands communicate? The nails constrict movement, but not completely.*

Sculpting these panels became my internal meditation, and as I prayed it became His visual communication.
I strongly felt that there should not be an impression of the cross in the crucifixion panels. Historically speaking, this sign had extremely negative associations for the Jewish people, and I sensed the focus had to be on the crucifixion and not on the cross.
The figure representing the crucified Lord emerged from within the wall made with highly textured Jerusalem stone, which has its own, distinct texture. The figure was in, and a part of, the wall to such a degree that the lines of the blocks went right through the body.

Because the crucified figure is so deeply immersed in the stones it give the impression that it is divided in two.

Likewise, the figures representing the Holocaust also became an ongoing meditation. I began to discover that the body stances created for the figure representing John also became the body communication for the Holocaust figures.

The Lord had known from the beginning what these figures would be saying. It took us years to understand the layers of communication in each one of the Holocaust sculptures.

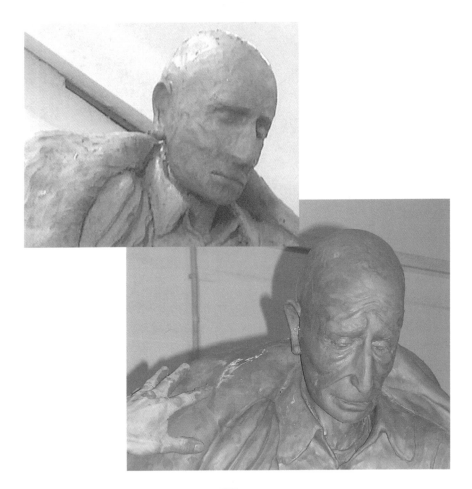

CHAPTER 33

Encounter with the Model
of the Holocaust

Because the image had changed from John the disciple to a person representing the Holocaust, I had to find a new model.

Yad Vashem, the Holocaust memorial museum in Jerusalem, has a large photo archive with almost two and a half million digital pictures. Some were donated from personal albums and others were taken by Allied soldiers, the Nazis or the Russian army.

For two and a half hours I watched the computer screen, looking for a specific face that could symbolize or be a model for the Holocaust figure within this work. It was very hard to look at those pictures, because they pulled me into a world of darkness and pain that I only knew superficially.

Suddenly a face appeared on the screen. Framed from the waist up, the picture of a very thin man, a blanket wrapped around his shoulders, looked straight at me. His terribly sad face was worn and lined, and he looked so tired. But it was his eyes that touched me deeply. Despite his exhaustion, I seemed to notice a flicker of life, and I could imagine him being able to tell me many stories.

That's him! I knew he would be my model.

The Yad Vashem worker made a photocopy for me to take home but could not provide me with any basic information such as his name, where he was from or how old he was.

For the next nine months, while creating the Holocaust's responses to the seven last words, I began to get to know the face beyond the photo. I tried to pull him off the page, to make him three-dimensional. Each of the seven Holocaust figures was sculpted with my photocopied picture close-by. Each response demanded another body stance and a different facial expression.

ABELS GESICHTER · I VOLTI DI ABELE

I created his expressions by guessing the way his facial lines would shift when he cried out, or when he was in deep despair, fearful or angry. I spent so many hours with this face that I knew every line and every possible muscle movement. Because the photocopy never changed, this always gave me a starting point. As the finished pieces began to fill my studio, he was everywhere.

When I was about to do the final phrase, "Into your hands I commend my spirit", I received a phone call from a German woman I knew who lived in Jerusalem. Many times she had organized trips to Poland to visit the six main Nazi extermination camps. Knowing that I was working on a piece related to the Holocaust, she thought I might be interested in joining them. By now I had been buried for months within this meditation, and the model from the black and white photocopy had been transformed into six life-size figures, each with its expression. It seemed like a good idea to take a short break and continue to mediate on the final sculpture while visiting the different concentration camps.

Our group met in Oswiecim, the Polish name for Auschwitz, where the camp was located. Our tour began at Auschwitz-Birkenau, the largest and most infamous of the Nazi extermination camps. Even though the Nazis had hundreds of concentration camps all over Europe, the six extermination camps had all been in Poland. Before we visited the Auschwitz camp museum, they showed us a fifteen-minute documentary film about the history and construction of the camp.

As I expected, the atmosphere in the room was heavy. The old black and white film, narrated in English, was compiled from Nazi footage and archived pictures. The last part contained Russian footage, as they had been the ones to liberate the camp in January, 1945. During that fierce winter in January, most of the prisoners had been forced on death marches towards Germany. The ones that had been left behind were often sick, but a few had managed to hide.
The Russians liberating the camp were filming everything they were discovering. I could almost feel the emotions of the cameraman exposing the horror they found.

When they came into Birkenau, for some reason the filming stayed focused on the back of one of the wooden barracks. The door of the barracks opened and a man stepped out and started to walk towards the camera. As he came closer the camera framed him about half body so you could really see his face. For about ten seconds the prisoner was filmed speaking. When I first looked at this prisoner's face, a piercing thought came into my head, *I know this man!* But then I argued, *How could I know someone from 1945 being discovered as a prisoner hiding in Birkenau?* Despite this fact I somehow knew him. Thoughts spinning, I kept thinking, *How can this be? Who does he remind me of?* All of a sudden it came crashing into my mind: *This is my model! This is him! This is the same man, this is the same face that I have been so carefully studying for almost a year!*
I wanted to scream, to yell, "I know him! I know every line in his face, every one of them!"
For a long time the camera stayed on him, and he even spoke to the cameraman; but because the black and white film had no audio, I couldn't hear what he said, except for seeing his mouth move. I wanted to say something back to him, but the film ended.

Dazed, I didn't know what to do. I wanted to watch the film again, but we had to leave. I couldn't explain what I felt to the others in my group. They wouldn't be able to understand it if I told them that I had seen someone I know but didn't know. That I spent large amounts of time with a person who until now had been a face on a piece of paper, smeared with clay and fingerprints.

During the rest of the day all kinds of thoughts raced through my mind. *He survived! Survived Auschwitz! But what was his name? Where did he go after the war? Did he move to Israel? Did he have children? Could they be living in the same town that I live in?*
All those questions intermingled with what I now saw at the camp, the place he had survived against all odds. Who could have guessed the probability that out of two and a half million pictures at Yad Vashem, representing thousands of different places and times, I would see this same face in an introduction film at the Auschwitz museum?

It was unbelievable, but for God nothing was impossible. I knew that if God allowed me to "meet" this man, I had to find out his name, and where he ended up after the war. The only fact I learned from the film was that he had been forty-two years old at the time of the liberation.

Since that time I have been to Auschwitz many, many times and have gotten to know some of the people working in the museum office, a few historians and the man in charge of the archives. By going through the names that were recorded by the Russians, we've narrowed down the list to 120 men who would have been 42 years old at that time. I have sent the film fragment of the talking man to a school for the deaf in Poland, asking if someone could read his lips and find out what he was saying. If he spoke Polish, that too would narrow down my search.

Everyone at the Auschwitz museum has been very helpful and patient with my search.

"It's like trying to find a needle in a haystack," they kept saying.

"But at least I have found there is a haystack," I told them.

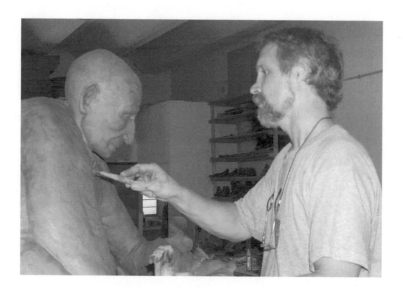

Benjamin Netanyahu visits Cadim during the disengagement talks

CHAPTER 34

Redeployment
and a Voice Crying in the Wilderness

Coming back to the settlement after the trip to Poland, things had changed, gotten deeper. I was relating to now to a real person and not just a photo, as I sculpted the final figure symbolizing the Holocaust in clay.

Already for years, Cadim members were constantly talking about the question of disengagement – yes or no? Both Prime Minister Yitzchak Rabin and later Ariel Sharon gave opposite messages. We felt thrown back and forth like a tennis ball. The tension of the unknown future also influenced our practical decisions. Do we put in new kitchen cabinets? Do we develop the house? Should we bother? We may not be living here much longer.

When Ariel Sharon became the Israeli Prime Minister, everyone in Cadim thought we were safe and could finally relax, but then suddenly everything changed. Totally unexpected, the government began to talk about redeployment of settlements, and Cadim was one of them.

While working on the "Fountain", although I didn't say it out loud, I had been thinking that my studio would not be big enough for this large piece. The first crucifixion panel I worked on was "My God My God why have You forsaken me?". I fastened it on a chipboard wall so that I could see the dimensions and have an idea what it would feel like full size. I didn't think a lot about money, I felt like I was responding to the Lord. He showed and confirmed to me that I was going the right direction, even if I didn't have any idea to where this was all leading.

2003 was the year of the beginning of the development of life size clay models of the crucifixion figures, at the same time working on two commissions – one in Europe (Basel, "Esther") and one in the USA (Indiana, "The Prodigal Son"). These two commissions brought in enough money that the following year 2004 I could work full time on the life size models for the Holocaust.

I was preparing the Holocaust clay sculptures for casting into bronze. This part demanded a lot of money but again, I wasn't really thinking about it. After Auschwitz and what God had given me there I was driven to just keep going.

By 2005 it was certain that redeployment would take place, so collectively the members of our settlement asked lawyers to represent us along with another settlement. Because of their experience with Yamit, the lawyers knew which papers to prepare ahead of time; so when the time came, they would be the first to apply for government compensation. This way, we would have the best chance of getting any compensation money. Those who waited too long would receive nothing, as the budget would have been gone by then. We were to receive 75% of the compensation money, and if we could prove a physical presence at a new address, we were to receive the other 25%.

Spring, 2005, when praying where the Lord wanted us to move to next, the word "Judah" kept coming to mind and also "A voice crying in the wilderness". I looked up the geographic area of the tribe of Judah on a Biblical map and immediately noticed that Jerusalem was part of it. However, the compensation money was not enough to buy an apartment in Jerusalem.

Before we came to live in the settlement the Lord had made it clear that we were never to go into debt. When we bought the house in Cadim, I had asked the Lord about entering into a mortgage situation, as then we would be in debt. The Lord told us then, that if we went into debt in obedience to Him, we would only be in debt to Him.

So now I was asking Him about our search for a new house: do we go back to the no-debt principle or are we able to use a mortgage again? *Back to the no-debt principle,* I felt the Lord saying.

Knowing that we had to buy a house, straight cash and no mortgage Dafna and I agreed not to expect the government to pay the last 25%; therefore, we should buy a house in the price range of the 75% compensation money. We soon found out that the only place which had affordable houses in that price range was the northern Negev, still Judah but not Jerusalem. In the end, the government did pay the last 25% of compensation and this covered the cost of all the casting of the bronze for the Holocaust figures.

For us, the time was perfect to buy a house in the Negev because the market was low, people were eager to sell and willing to work out a deal.

"Lord," I prayed, "I need a house with a studio AND a wall at least 53 feet long." I calculated that length would be needed for the finished "Fountain of Tears".

We knew a realtor who lived in the Northern Negev in Arad, a small city. We decided to drive down and meet with her and get a general idea of the area.

"I'm handling many houses," the realtor said, "and happen to be on my way to check one in Arad. Perhaps you would like to see it?"

While the realtor showed Dafna around the house, I wandered around to the back and discovered an L-shaped courtyard. One part of the "L" had a storage space. *That could be my studio*, I thought.

Turning the corner, I stepped into an open courtyard with a long wall, on one side. Looking at the structure, I thought, *Here's the wall! I wonder how long it is?* Even though I had told the Lord that I roughly needed 53 ft., this wall happened to be 60 ft. *Wow!* I thought. *If this is the Lord, then He is being generous!* (Eventually, I did need the full length of the wall for the finished "Fountain".) Letting my eyes wander through the courtyard, I thought, *I really hope Dafna likes the house, because I'm buying this wall!*

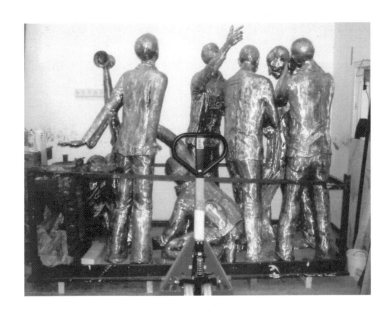

142

In July, 2005, our final date for leaving our houses was set - July 27. Families could leave before that date, but on July 27 the settlement had to be completely empty.

We were leaving with a lot of mixed feelings. We had been friends with just about everyone on the settlement and had lived out our lives as believers before them. We had done a lot of things that they didn't understand, but there had been a mutual respect. We had never chased them but waited for them to ask questions about our relationship with Jesus. We had had some great dialogues and interactions with them.

Both our boys had grown up there and they would carry a lot of childhood memories of their life on the settlement.

The Lord had established this time as an intercession that we were to live. Now it was the beginning of another intercession that had been developing since the 'Pay Back' word and establishing our lives in Arad with the "Fountain of Tears". We were glad to go.

Because of the studio, our family was given an extension to the deadline, till August 15. For seven out of the twelve years that we had lived on the settlement I had a large space in the industrial area that I used for a studio. I had accumulated a lot of tools and materials over the years, but the largest of all to move was the beginning elements of the "Fountain".

Those last weeks I worked hard to weld all the pieces of the Holocaust figures together. That July we moved house, the studio in the beginning of August. My kibbutz father asked a truck driver from the kibbutz to come with a gigantic, flatbed, transport truck with an 80 ton crane to help transport the studio. Daniel, who was in the army then, received a special two-week leave to help me construct wooden crates and then pack them.

143

These were then lifted by crane on the truck. Leaving the settlement for the last time was strange for both Dafna and I. We now felt no emotions, we were looking forward.

The move to Arad created the wall I needed for the "Fountain" and for the construction of all that was still needed. The idea of using Jerusalem stone in the crucifixion scenes was born here. What had been the construction zone of the "Fountain" eventually became the exhibition room where we now receive visitors.

CHAPTER 35

Gethsemane

Slowly I began to see the crucifixion and the Holocaust coming together. It became a dialogue of suffering between these two personalities, both carrying such deep pain, yet both being so deeply estranged from each other historically. Could there be common ground between them? Had there been a fellowship of suffering? I didn't know, but perhaps they would talk to me while I created them. But in order to do so, I had to go back to the beginning – to Gethsemane.

There is so much attached to this word "Gethsemane": it is a place of darkness, filled with horror and an intense struggle of wills. But it is also a garden where olives are harvested and crushed to bring out oil, used in Bible times for healing, for anointing of kings. In this darkest of all nights, the will to live was crushed and pressed in order to give the oil of life, crushed, not simply by dying, which might have eased the struggle, but by way of a slow, methodically crafted torture. This was a death designed to inflict the maximum amount of pain for the longest possible time.

In a small way the Gethsemane sculpture reflected how I felt before creating the "Fountain of Tears". It was such a struggle to start this God-ordained commission. I knew it would cost me everything, that I might lose all my friends. It had been a miracle that I, the Gentile, had received Israeli citizenship – a sign from heaven I was to stay in Israel, to become a part, to learn the language. I had joined the kibbutz, served in the IDF. God had given me a love for these people; the relationships that had been forged reflected God's hand on it all. It was such an honor to be part of this people. Was there a possibility I could lose it all? The Holocaust was one of the deepest threads running through the fabric of this country.

Touching this subject almost felt like entering something so holy that it was better avoided. It was a place one approached with questions, but never with answers.

How could I connect the terrible memories of the Holocaust to Jesus' crucifixion and His last seven words? My Israeli friends would be infuriated that I, the Gentile claiming to be their friend, dared to create a dialogue between those two events that only cursed each other. *Can there be a dialogue reflecting each other's pain?* I wondered. *Can there be a fellowship of suffering between the two that will bring a cleansing and healing to all this misunderstanding and deep hatred?*

The struggle with this commission was like a personal Gethsemane to me; my own justifications and those self-preserving arguments had to die; now I had to begin sculpting. I was reminded of Jeremiah 9,

"Oh Lord that my head was a spring of water and my eyes a fountain of tears, that I would weep day and night for the lost of my people."

Knowing that this journey was not just the sculpting of a large project but a journey of prayer and intercession, I wondered where to start. Gethsemane, perhaps? In a sense, that was where the crucifixion began. In this place, the Father showed the Son what lay in front of Him.

The Holocaust - could this garden scene resemble all those nights in which the Jewish people were rounded up and sent to prisons or camps? For Jesus it was the night of His captivity, when they bound him and led Him away. Different steps had been taken between the time of His imprisonment and His final judgment. After a lot of political maneuvering and manipulations came the final solution - His death by crucifixion. The Jewish people were first bound by the Nuremberg Laws and then led into captivity to the ghettos until the SS put the final solution into action, death in the gas chambers, crucifixion.

I sculpted the Jesus figure as being poured out over a large stone, as if His body took on the very shape of the stone.

The focus of His struggle is represented in the cup of suffering which He holds, allegorically pictured in the shape of a cup that is filled to the brim with suffering. As the Father showed the Son everything that was in the cup, His sweat mixed with drops of blood flowed over the stone. Would He even have known that there would be a moment of total abandonment by the Father? And then the Father asked His Son to drink of this horror for the sake of salvation for those who had been the very ones to persecute and hate Him.

In the sculpture Jesus holds the cup in His left hand, fully extending His arm, as far away from His mouth as possible. The cup is balanced between His index finger and thumb, while the other three fingers are free from holding it. This symbolizes Jesus' indecision, the three fingers representing the three times He called to His disciples to pray with Him but found them asleep.

Three times He prayed to the Father that the cup would be removed from Him. In that darkest of all nights He alone made the terrible decision, "Father, if it is Your will, take this cup from me, nevertheless not my will, but Your will be done."

The crucifixion began the moment Jesus agreed to drink the cup of suffering.

CHAPTER 36

Two Evil Designs for a Violent Death

Neither crucifixion nor the Holocaust were natural causes of death; in fact, each of them had been well-thought-out, designed to inflict the maximum amount of pain, both ending in violent death. In the first case, Jesus was put on trial, accused and condemned for being the King of the Jews. In the case of the Holocaust, being Jewish already meant the death sentence. In a similar pattern, both died and were buried and were resurrected. While Jesus was buried for three days, the Jews were buried for three years. Jesus' resurrection created a heavenly kingdom, while the resurrection of the Jewish people created a nation.

I began to ponder. On this level there seemed to be a connection of suffering between the crucifixion and the Holocaust. Could there be a more intimate link between the seven last words and the Holocaust? How do these specific words from the crucifixion speak to the Holocaust? Where is the identification, if there is one at all? Am I on some strange creative journey leading to nowhere?

I knew that I would need to prayerfully struggle over each word. I would have to draw inspiration, not from my personal memory of suffering, but from within the heart of the Father. His memory was filled with the last cries of His Son and the tears of each and every Jewish victim that died during the Holocaust. He remembered each spot where a man, woman or child had been murdered.

I would not dare to presume that through this work I understood the pain of both Jesus and the Jewish people, but I knew that God had given me permission to create this piece. I began to hear the Father's heart and, therefore, had been able to identify with them.

Those seven words – they had to be taken one at a time because each word would become part of my life. From the moment I woke up, I began to think about a specific phrase and pondered upon it while I kneaded the moist clay around the metal armature that eventually would become a life-size figure.

The words floated in and out of my mind while I tried to solve a technical problem or sculpt an area that needed adjusting. Working the material was great, because it became a time of true meditation. Usually I worked in silence for hours with the material that was so giving and obliging.

Gradually the clay became a shape in which I recognized my thoughts, my feelings and my prayers. Above all, I hoped it would also communicate His prayers and His Heart, for only then would my work become an act of intercession. Dafna and I knew that this creative, intercessory process would reflect Jeremiah's words and that somehow this would also touch the 'payback' word. We didn't quite know how, but there had always been many more unknowns to us than known.

Jeremiah's tears were symbolized by water slowly dripping over the six fieldstone columns that joined the seven panels into one long wall. At the bottom of each pillar the water was collected and channeled underground to six olive trees outside the courtyard, facing the desert. Those trees represented the prophetic "payback" word, and the water represented the life-giving tears shed over the six million who perished in the Holocaust.

The last words Jesus spoke during the crucifixion would be so very important, as they were to be His last public communication to both Jews and Gentiles. The "King of the Jews" sign heralded the first, written, public statement about Him. By giving His life in this final act of intercession, He would be given the Father's seal of authority, not only as King of Kings but also as King of the Jews – King of His own brothers.

The bronze figures representing the Holocaust survivors each carried their visual marks. Everything was intended to dehumanize the Jewish people so they were indistinguishable from one another; their very humanity became unrecognizable.

Many people refused to see what was happening to the Jews; they turned their heads so they wouldn't see them being marched into the ghettos or loaded into cattle cars and, finally, locked up in concentration camps. Likewise, people turned their faces so they would not have to look at Jesus; after having received so many beatings, He had also become unrecognizable.

Through body language – either by his facial expression or the way he holds his hands - the Holocaust figure responds to the word spoken by the crucified One. The way he touches the stone pillars evokes the memory of those who perished. Only much later did we discover that the dark brown stones we had chosen to make the pillars were called "burnt stones" only found in the northern Negev region. When this dark, very hard stone becomes wet, it turns the same amber color as the bronze figures.

CHAPTER 37

The Face of a Sad Angel

Before and during the time I worked on the "Fountain", I read many books related to the Holocaust. The book that most affected me was *Night* by Elie Wiesel. For me, one of the strongest paragraphs in the book was in the foreword by Francois Mauriac. During that time I was in the preliminary phase of the "Fountain" and desperately looking for something that could help me begin the creative process.
This is what I read:

> "On that most horrible day, even among all those other bad days, when the child (Elie Wiesel) witnessed the hanging (yes!) of another child who, he tells us, had the face of a sad angel, he heard someone behind him groan: 'For God's sake, where is God?'
>
> "And from within me, I heard a voice answer: 'Where He is? This is where - hanging here from this gallows.'
>
> "...And I, who believe that God is love, what answer was there to give my young interlocutor whose dark eyes still held the reflection of the angelic sadness that had appeared one day on the face of a hanged child? What did I say to him? Did I speak to him of that other Jew, this crucified Brother who perhaps resembled him and whose cross conquered the world? Did I explain to him that what had been a stumbling block for his faith had become a cornerstone for mine? And that the connection between the cross and human suffering remains, in my view, the key to the unfathomable mystery in which the faith of his childhood was lost. And yet, Zion has risen up again out of the crematoria and the slaughterhouses. The Jewish nation has been resurrected from among its thousands of dead. It is they who have given it new life. We do not know the worth of one single drop of blood, one single tear. All is grace. If the Almighty is the Almighty, the last word for each of us belongs to Him. That is what I should have said to the Jewish child, but all I could do was embrace him and weep."

The book *Night* by Elie Wiesel was for me such a strong personal presentation of the journey of a fourteen-year-old boy into the darkness of the Holocaust. The Holocaust had to be seen through the eyes of one person in order to somehow touch the number six million. But the words from Francois Mariac in the introduction of the book identified my own personal dilemma; like him, I would not be able to give words, but only embraces and tears. All the drawings that I had done in my hope to find a starting place now had to be left behind. I had to embrace the clay and the tears that I would encounter would be my real points of reference within this journey. The tears demanded that I respond by going into a place of darkness that I didn't understand, but I had to go.

The creative process was like entering into a prayer, but its beginning was not from within me. Like the deluge of tears that invaded that moment with the 'payback' word, this interaction also seemed detached from me. My life in following Jesus had never been based on the knowing of a thing, but on a response to what I was sensing from Him. Knowledge, at least in part, seemed to come to me later each time. There was not always an understanding, but there was a sense of His presence. His presence seemed to be marked in tears, tears of such deep pain sorrow, it scared me, but not enough to cause me to refuse. This was to be His memory and not mine; He had made that clear. How deep the pain would be, how I would carry it, I didn't know, but again I had to respond.

Now was the time to enter into those seven last words of Jesus. These would be the doorways.

As I began to see there was a link between Jesus and the Holocaust victim even in these beginning steps, I became intrigued.
"Father forgive them, they don't know what they do".
Here was forgiveness, not spewed out words of hatred towards those that had nailed him to this cross, not a curse nor a hope of revenge, but a prayer, an intercession for the killers, a beseeching of the Father to show mercy to the murderers, because they did not know what they had done.

The more I thought about this, the more I was amazed.
This forgiveness was not coming out of the nature of a man, but was a reflection of a Son that had aligned His life to his Father's.

How could I show this in the clay? This prayer asking for forgiveness was not just weakly uttered words, but was a declaration, almost a shout, a shout that defined His own life, and more, it was the beginning of a covenant.
This covenant would be solely founded on forgiveness, even for the most unforgiveable.

CHAPTER 38

"Father, forgive them!"

No one knows the order of the words spoken at the time of the crucifixion, but I imagined those words, "Father, forgive them!", to be first and foremost on the mind of Jesus.

This, I felt, should be the first panel, as the crucifixion itself is an act of bringing forgiveness. The Lamb of God was slaughtered in order to create a covenant of forgiveness. I believe that not only did He forgive those who crucified Him, those who caused it to happen and the Roman soldier who drove the nails into His hands and feet, but that Jesus turned this forgiveness into a covenant, a new covenant, into a way of life for those who followed Him.

I sculpted the figure of Jesus crucified with His head forward and His face intentional. He is not focused on the physical pain, but on the declaration He makes, "Father, forgive them!" By uttering those words, He created the covenant. And His hands, even though nailed to the wood, are held wide open as He continues to give to those who can and are willing to receive.

The figure representing the Holocaust turns towards the pillar of stones as if he is leaning into those who perished. He wrestles with this word of forgiveness, because this covenant demands that when we receive forgiveness, we must also forgive others. Receiving forgiveness is shown by the Holocaust figure as he grips his chest with one hand while the other hand is turned outward, resting on the stone pillar, as if he is giving forgiveness out.

But how can he forgive those perpetrators, the murderers of those who died, while he continues to live? He struggles. His life is attached to the stones of the perished, interwoven with them. His greatest fear is that the moment he forgives, those who perished will be forgotten.

If that happened, they would be betrayed twice.

"Never forgive, never forget" is a generally accepted statement in Israel concerning the Holocaust. It is almost as if when "forgiveness" is considered, the Jewish people think that the immediate result will be "forgetting."

One day I met Martin, a Holocaust survivor who soon after the war had immigrated to the States. Martin and his wife now lived in the Denver area, and they had become friends with Christian Zionists who invited them to many pro-Israel events in their church. Throughout the years, Martin had become an honored friend of that Christian community. One day, Martin confided to his friends that he suffered from recurrent nightmares in which he relived the horrors of the different camps that he had survived. Those memories left him in a state of turmoil.

"We can pray for you, Martin," the couple offered. "God can heal you. Then, those nightmares won't trouble you any longer."

"Oh, please, don't!" Martin pleaded with them. "If you pray for me, I know these nightmares will stop. Please don't!"

"But, why?" The couple was shocked by his response.

"Because this is my only connection to those I have lost," he said. "And even though the memory of those who died is still so painful, I cannot disconnect myself from them. They continue to live on in my memories, and I will always carry them with me, even if the memories produce nightmares."

"Father, forgive them, for they know not what they do" – this is the first record of Jesus asking the Father directly to forgive. Usually it was Jesus himself who spoke words of forgiveness, greatly angering the religious of His time. Maybe the crucifixion and the Holocaust are connected by the fact that no human being is able to forgive both atrocities – no one but the Father.

Does the Holocaust survivor have a wrong concept of the word forgiveness? A wrong concept of remembering?
Has he perhaps embraced a lie?

For me, it is shocking to find a church who claims Jesus as Lord, blatantly ignoring His prayer to forgive those who crucified Him. Historically, the church branded the Jews as Christ killers, as if the words "Father, forgive them" could never include the Jews. Have they also embraced a lie?

My head was filled with thoughts and questions as I walked through this first word. Would all of the seven words provoke such a mental

160

CHAPTER 39

"Today you will be with Me in Paradise." Luke 23:43

I love the words, "Today you will be with Me in Paradise", for these are the words spoken to a desperate, dying man. His request only to be remembered, followed by Jesus' response, destroys all doctrines and dictates that we have created as prerequisites for entrance into salvation, as if we were the custodians of salvation.

"Lord, when you come into your Kingdom, please remember me," is all the thief asks of Jesus. "Please, don't forget me!"

Hanging to the left of Jesus is the other thief. In his last minutes of life, he is mocking and cursing. I sculpted the left hand of the crucifixion as turned down, turned away; this is not a show of judgment, but a sign of disappointment. This thief forgets that he is a man who needs God.

The heart of the Father beating in Jesus' chest is drawn to the thief on the right who remembered who he was. The figure of the crucifixion turns hard toward the right, even though His body is constricted by the nails. The crucifixion figure's right hand is trying to touch the stone pillar as a picture of God reaching out to all those who called to Him, asking to be remembered, even in the last moments of life.

I am trying within this piece to reflect Jesus' heart, which is the Father heart of God. "Father"– this word carries authority.
If in the last moments of life Jesus heard the cry of a thief asking to be remembered, how much more would God the Father reach out to His own people. Their cries from within the Holocaust had to have pulled Him to try and touch their suffering. I began to think that God as Father could not forget them. He would have to respond or He would have been denying His own role as Father. These thoughts gave me hope.

The figure representing the Holocaust stands erect with his hands pointing in two different directions. Is he identifying with the crucifixion, or is he hearing his own words out of the mouths of these two thieves?

Having heard the story of the two thieves from me, a Holocaust survivor also echoed what the last words of those two crucified men had been, one thief cursing Jesus, the other begging to be remembered.

"I can identify with both thieves," the survivor responded. "In Auschwitz we daily lived within an inch of death. With the little strength we had left, there were days when we cursed and mocked God. But there were also days when we cried out to Him, begging Him to remember us."

What she had said amazed me; yes, on one hand cursing and mocking, but on the other hand, so wanting to be remembered, so wanting to touch life.
That is why the hands of the Holocaust figure point in opposite directions. The one reaching upward to the right identifies with Jesus' hand that gives life, while the second hand, going in the opposite direction, recognizes the thief who mocks and curses.

CHAPTER 40

"Mother, this is your son; son, this is your mother." John 19:26-27

From the viewpoint of the crucifixion, the words "Mother, this is your son; son, this is your mother," are easy to understand because they so much reflect Jesus' heart. In the deepest pain, amidst His own suffering, He cares for His mother. In this panel I searched for a way to show Jesus putting her on the shoulder of a friend, someone He trusted - John, His beloved friend and the only disciple staying with Him throughout the crucifixion.

Jesus entrusts and commits His mother into the care of John, who now had to support and carry her as if she was his own mother. By doing what He did, Jesus passed His earthly role as a son onto his friend. This unnatural relationship between John and Mary was created from a place of suffering.
The way John had been given the responsibility to look after Mary from that moment, could this be similar to what the Holocaust survivors felt in taking on the responsibility towards those who had perished?
This is symbolized by the figure of the Holocaust carrying a heavy cloth on his shoulder. Within the folds of this material, one can see the figure of an emaciated and surreal woman. The survivor is carrying "her" in one arm; the interwoven body is draped over his shoulders and the end of the cloth is held in his hand. He experiences a similar kind of relationship with the memories of the dead, yet they are like a heavy weight because it is an unnatural relationship. The majority of his family was killed, but in their place he now carries and identifies with the memories of six million people. This unnatural relationship is more intimate than any he has known before. He stares at the end of the cloth in his hand.

The end of the cloth in the hand of the Holocaust figure represents the

 realization of what personally happened to him. The cloth moves up his arm and widens as he begins to comprehend the devastation and loss of his relatives and family, then the cloth takes on the form of a woman as he realizes the loss of his village and, finally, of the country he had belonged to.

This is shown by the women-shaped cloth draped over his shoulder which then falls to the ground.

The back, buttocks and legs of the figure of the bronze, naked woman merges with the six very pronounced folds which relate to the six million. He will bear the memory of this new and unnatural relationship for the rest of his life.

Throughout the years we have shown the "Fountain" to many people, but when I host Holocaust survivors I always feel intimidated by them. I have created this work through my relationship with the crucifixion and the Holocaust, but the survivor carries the memory with him. It is part of who he is and who he has become. One day a friend of mine brought a visitor. Sarah, in her late seventies, looked like a classic grandmother, her hair neatly arranged and her dress a little formal. I learned only later that she was born in the Netherlands and starting at the age of four had been hidden by different families for the duration of the war. At the end of the war, eight-year-old Sarah was the sole survivor of her large family.

Standing next to her in front of the panels, I began by explaining to Sarah how I had created the "Fountain". I felt nervous, especially because she remained so quiet. She didn't look at me while I spoke, but looked intently at the sculpture.

When we came to the third panel "Mother, this is your son; son, this is your mother" she turned to me, looked me in the eyes and said,

"How did you know? How did you know I've been carrying this cloak on my heart for all these years? How could you possibly have known?"

I didn't know how to respond, for she was right to be asking me this question. How could I know? I had no personal memory or experience of the Holocaust. That would have been impossible with my background.

"I didn't know, but God does!" was all I said. "If I had a choice, I would have run from this project, but He didn't let me."

CHAPTER 41

"My God, my God! Why have you forsaken me?" Mark 15:34

As I approached the next word, I sensed a fear, a foreboding, a cry of abandonment from a son that had enjoyed the presence of God more than anyone ever would. *"My God, my God, why have you forsaken me?"* How could I sculpt this? This would be the hardest panel of the seven. Out of these seven last words, this word would be the deepest place of pain. It would be the place of abandonment so deep that God could not be found or somehow felt. This would be the word to which the constant question "Where was GOD?" is attached.

I started with the figure in the crucifixion, Jesus as the son feeling the loss of the Father's presence. The cry must have been terrible.
I sculpted the head as far back as I could with the mouth wide open, everything pointing upward. The lips extended, searching for the last breath. Not being able to feel the presence of the Father at this point during the crucifixion must have been the last thing Jesus could ever have imagined would happen to Him.

In Gethsemane did the Father let Jesus know fully what lay before him in the crucifixion? Did he know that the Father would intentionally abandon him? Was this the point in Gethsemane when Jesus sweated blood? This cry in the crucifixion had to go upward, the words themselves searching but not finding.
I thought even the beginning words, "My God, My God," showed a level of the desertion. When had Jesus ever referred to God as God? He had always spoken of God as Father.

While working on the piece, I went to see a close friend, a Jewish believer who had lost family members in the Holocaust. When I told him that I was really struggling with this word, "My God, my God, why have you forsaken me?", he gave me a book that was written by a member of the Sonderkommando. These were men in special units, mostly made up of Jewish prisoners in the Nazi death camps. Threatened to be killed themselves, they were forced to "facilitate the lie". They had to tell those getting out of the train cars that this was just a stop and they were going now to take a shower. The men of the Sonderkommando could usually speak Yiddish and could help calm the fears and questions of those being led to the slaughter of the gas chambers.

The man writing the book gave testimony that the gassing process would take twenty minutes. For the first ten minutes he could hear the cries and prayers rising up in the gas chamber as people were dying, until the gas finally silenced the screams. He said even now that as an old man he could never forget the screams, that they would forever be with him. He then referred to hearing over and over again from within the dying voices a cry from the beginning verses of Psalm 22, "My God, my God, why have you forsaken me?"

This stunned me, this man giving a personal account revealing that the same words cried out then from the gas chambers were exactly what I was working on now as the cry of Jesus in His last minutes of life. I had not realized that these same words were in the Psalms; I had thought that they had belonged only to Jesus during the crucifixion. The identification to both the crucifixion and the Holocaust was so exact that it shifted how I would sculpt this.
I felt strongly that both the figures of the Holocaust and the crucifixion would have to look alike as much as possible. I knew when sculpting the Holocaust survivor that I had three visional marks that I could use: the shaved head, the striped clothes and the tattooed prisoner number. While sculpting the head for the crucifixion I realized that the head had to be shaved and there was to be no beard.

In a sense Jesus was beginning to identify fully with the Jews in the Holocaust, and I felt fear about this, as if I was entering a place of deep intimacy in which I was sure I did not belong, yet into which I had to go.

I was being led towards the tattooed number, that ultimate connection of the survivor to this hell of the Holocaust, that place of memory that would never go away. The hair could grow back after the camps and they could burn their striped clothes, but the number would always remain burned into their bodies. This number would have the ability to take a survivor back to the memories of the camps within an instant.
I had known survivors who, in coming to Israel after the war, had always worn long sleeved shirts to cover up the number, so no one would see it and ask questions.

I have a friend both of whose parents survived Auschwitz. She was a single child that had grown up, as she put it, with ghosts, with all of her relatives that she had never met and had died, but were in many ways always living with her parents. Her mother would make a point of talking to her about the Holocaust, which is uncharacteristic. Her father was almost totally silent in every way, except for the crying in the night, that she would hear. She told me that she could never show emotions as a little girl, because she knew they couldn't handle it. When she was four years old, she had realized that the reason that her father couldn't speak and was always so sad was because of the number tattooed on his arm. She asked him if she could wash it away and he agreed. She tried for a long time and with many types of soap, but the number remained. It would always remain.

I knew that I had to put a number on Jesus' arm; there had to be full identification with the victims of the Holocaust. I knew what a number meant in the eyes of survivors and their children. I knew this as I put a number on the figure of the crucified Jesus, an image which carries so many negative memories for the Jewish people.
How could I dare touch this level of pain? This was the worst moment of the entire seven year process of creating the "Fountain".

But I knew I had to do it, for the figure of Jesus and the Holocaust survivor had to look exactly the same.

When showing the "Fountain" to groups, I was asked by some people why I chose to put the number 1534 on the arm. Even though they would not understand my emotional struggle with this panel, I usually tried to explain how hard it had been for me to put the number there and how eventually I had decided on the number 1534 because one and five makes six, thus reflecting the six million Jews that perished, and three and four makes seven, which relates to the last seven words of the crucifixion.

"Perhaps there is another meaning for this number," people suggested.

"Did something significant happen to the Jewish people in the year 1534?" someone asked.

"Perhaps the number has something to do with Jesus' disciples when they had been fishing all night and caught nothing?" another said. "Jesus told them to throw the net on the other side and they caught 153 fishes."

"What about the number four, then?" I would ask.

"Well, you probably messed up on that one," the person said. When sharing my "Fountain" journey with groups, I often just tried to be polite and let the people read into it what they wanted, knowing that they didn't understand the emotions of doing it, until the day I told a friend of all the speculations, and he decided to add his own,

"Could it be perhaps be chapter and verse?" he suggested. "You know, a number of a chapter with the number of a Bible verse?"

Again, I tried to be polite and said, "Whatever."

"I have been searching and found something," my friend called me a few days later.

Having completely forgotten what the search was all about, I listened.

"I've searched through a number of Bible books until I came to Mark 15, verse 34," he said. "Do you know what's written there?" When he read the words, I was shocked!

"And at the ninth hour Jesus cried out with a loud voice, saying, *"Eloi, Eloi, lama sabachthani?"* which is translated, *"My God, my God! Why have you forsaken me?"*

Stunned, I realized that my randomly chosen number corresponded with those exact words in the Bible verse. Somehow, God Himself had marked these words.

I sculpted the figure representing the Holocaust with his arms thrown behind him and his body projected forward. On the faces of the victims of both the Holocaust and the crucifixion, there is the same expression, the same cry upward, the same desperation, the same last breath. This bronze Holocaust figure is the only one with his back turned to the crucifixion; both men are crying out but, separated, are alone. The body is thrown forward, in a way showing the cry "Where was God?" thrown through time. It has been proven historically that this was the cry from the gas chambers then. It is still the same cry now. The face of the Holocaust figure is almost a mirror image of the face of the crucified figure. Both men have the same cry; one, the crucified Jesus, is a son asking a genuine question; the other, the Holocaust victim, has turned his back in anger and is not asking, but is accusing.

CHAPTER 42

"I thirst!" John 19:28

When I began to approach the sculpting for "I thirst", I started thinking of Jesus when He made the declaration that He is living water, and that if any man comes unto Him and drinks, that man will not be thirsty anymore. But Jesus is now thirsty, so what does it mean? I began to think that if Jesus is a well of living water and now He is saying He thirsts, it must mean that all within Him has been given, all has been poured out.

I sculpted the head in the crucifixion looking down with its mouth open; the hands are surreal and the fingers are long and pointing down; the body is being pulled down and the feet are in the shape of a single droplet of water. I felt that everything had to be moving down-ward, and the feet were to be as the last droplet, even as the last tear.

This made me think of what survivors had said to me, that in order to survive in the camps, there could be no more human emotions, no more tears.

I thought of the characteristic of water, when poured out, is to find the lowest place possible. Everything in the sculpting was moving downward, so I put the figure representing the Holocaust in a crouched position. He is not kneeling, but crouching. I did not want this to look like he was kneeling before the crucifixion, but like he was identifying with his own tears, his own thirst.

Thirst had to be divided into two parts. One would be the physical part that brings death to the body; the other part would be the dryness of the soul that brings an inner death.

It is reported by those in the camps that you could survive for a long time on small portions of food, but without water you were dead in a short time. There were many compressed within the train cars on the way to the camps who had died from thirst. So the survivor could relate to the thirst that kills the body. The inner thirst comes when there are no more human emotions, no more tears. The camps would also take this away.

This is why the sculpture reflecting the Holocaust communicates with both hands. The one hand is down touching the ground, looking for the water that will satisfy the body; the other hand is almost touching the feet, the last tear, identifying with the thirst of the soul.

CHAPTER 43

"It is finished!" John 19:30

"It is finished" is a word that has so many levels of meaning. How do you sculpt this? Is Jesus bringing an end to His suffering? That in itself is amazing, because a crucifixion could last for days.

Did Jesus die more quickly because of the severity of the flogging He had received? The crucifixion took place prior to the Passover celebration. The Jewish rulers asked that the legs of the crucified men be broken so death would come quickly by suffocation. In this way those who were crucified would not be left hanging on the cross during the Passover feast. Being the Lamb of God, was Jesus meant to die before Passover began?

I decided that these words had to be another declaration, not just words spoken in a whisper. They had to be intentional, with force and focus.

So I sculpted the face looking straight out. The expression had to be strong and intentional. I put the fingers of the hands closed over the nails, so that the heads of the nails could not been seen. In this way, I was trying to say, "It is finished. But it is not just finished. I, Jesus, myself have brought it to an end." Jesus had given himself to the crucifixion in Gethsemane, and now with authority He was declaring its completion.

Now the figure of the Holocaust, how would he respond to this declaration? The largest Jewish population conquered by the Nazis had been there. Poland had been home for the Jews. There had been a full expression of Jewish culture in Poland for almost a thousand years; this culture was destroyed within the six years of the Holocaust. The destruction was so complete, it would never be what it had been before. It was finished.

The figure of the Holocaust represents Poland in 1945. In 1945, the only place on the planet that wanted Jews was Palestine. However, the British Mandate government did everything in its power to stop Jewish immigration. The Holocaust victim covers his face with one hand, showing a loss of identity; his other hand is raised up, almost trying to point in a direction with his index finger. Yet the finger is bent down, for there is no direction, no place to go. He has a history that he cannot see anymore and a future with no direction.
It is finished.

CHAPTER 44

"Into Your hands I commend my spirit."
Luke 23:46

"Into Your hands I commend my spirit" are the final words, the last utterances as Jesus delivers His spirit into the hands of the Father. With this piece, I had to sculpt the figure with nothing more to give. The body hangs at the lowest position of all the other crucifixion panels. All the breath has been taken, the fingers of the hands are pulled downward, the head is buried in His chest. The spirit has been given out.

How does the Holocaust victim give up his spirit, into whose hands does he deliver it? I felt that if the figure of the Holocaust in the previous panel represented 1945, this figure would represent the years between 1945 and 1948. In a way he would represent Jewish burial.
The bronze figure has fallen, collapsed and now lies on the ground. One hand is trying to touch the water that represents the tears on the pillar; the other arm is deciding whether to try and raise its body up or to fully lie down.

Over the figure is a heavy cloth, a mantle of death. Interwoven in the folds of the cloth is an emaciated body with its hands lying on the ground, face up.

Survivors I had known, after having been freed from the Nazi concentration camps in 1945, were placed back into displaced persons camps for almost three years. There they struggled over direction and identity. This was like being buried with the dead. Still in Europe, they did not know whether to fully lie in this grave or to try to push themselves up. The hands of the body in the cloth turned upward represent the dead saying to the living, "Into your hands we commend our spirit and our memory."

CHAPTER 45

"The Butterfly"

After death and burial, could there be resurrection?
The question that always seemed to be floating in the air was whether there could be a relationship between the crucifixion and the Holocaust? Could there be something in common with the sufferings of both? Death was obviously a part of both, but burial? There seemed to be a similarity in time. Jesus was buried for three days, the Jewish people for three years, from the spring of 1945 to the spring of 1948 when Israel became a nation of its own. Was this the end of burial and the beginning of resurrection?
During the working on the wall, these were only thoughts that I had had. The wall had become this dialogue of suffering between the crucifixion and Holocaust. But now, I was asking myself these broader questions.

I had created the 'Butterfly' during my work on the 'Fountain of Tears'. The child in the crematorium had been birthed out of a book and out of music. The book was *I Never Saw Another Butterfly*, a collection of Jewish children's poetry saved out of the Holocaust from a ghetto called Terezin (Theresienstadt). The majority of the children from Terezin themselves were not saved, but were killed in the gas chambers of Auschwitz-Birkenau. These short poems became their last words.

Sketch Butterfly piece

The first "Butterfly" piece accompanied Oratorio Terezin. After the three performances of the oratorio in Israel, the sculpture was given to the museum dedicated to the children from Terezin at Kibbutz Givat Haim. The second copy of the sculpture was done and intended for a museum in Europe, but in the end, this did not happen, and the piece stayed with me. It moved with us when we had had to leave Cadim.

When I started working on the wall for the "Fountain", it was always close at hand but almost like an onlooker. There was no thought that the "Butterfly" would become a part of the "Fountain".
But now as I started to come to the end of the wall and the dialogue between the Holocaust and the crucifixion, the question of resurrection was coming up. In looking at the piece of the "Butterfly", I began to see resurrection. The hand of the child going through the crematorium door and clutching a small piece of ground is resurrection.
That hand was the beginning of a resurrection of a people to a land. The child possesses it, holds on to it, but like the butterfly, he never sees it. Like the butterfly in the piece, the resurrection is just outside of the reach of the child; he can't even feel it, but it is his.

Olive leaves, representing olive oil, cover the ground. This oil, from a biblical point of view, was used for healing and anointing. This oil would be for Israel, rising now as a nation out of the ashes of the crematoriums; it would be for her healing, for her to know the anointing of God upon her.

While visiting Terezin in 2004, I walked from the main barracks to a wide open field that is marked as a mass grave. To commemorate those who perished, a large Star of David stands on one side while a large sculptured menorah stands on the other side. The Star of David stands over the unmarked stones placed randomly in the field.
In a far corner of the field is a small building that was used as a crematorium for those who had died within the Terezin camp.
A memorial marker says, "To whom it was not given to die in their own land."

The last, the very last,
So richly, brightly, dazzlingly yellow.
Perhaps if the sun's tears would sing
Against a white stone...
Such, such a yellow
Is carried lightly way up high.
It went away I'm sure because it wished to
Kiss the world goodbye.
For seven weeks I've lived in here,
Penned up inside this ghetto
But I have found my people here.
The dandelions call to me
And the white chestnut candles in the court.
Only I never saw another butterfly.
That butterfly was the last one.
Butterflies don't live in here,
In the ghetto.

Poem written by Pavel Friedmann on June 4, 1942.
He died in Auschwitz-Birkenau on September 29, 1944.

After reflecting on those words, I was stirred within, and I began to weep. "Their own land" kept rolling around in my head. Somehow the words touched an area which so much symbolized the Jewish people during that time, a people who did not even have their own homeland in which to be buried. But now they do.

I realized that this piece, the "Butterfly", would need to follow "Into your hands I commend my Spirit". The last two pieces would represent the two parts of resurrection, the land of the nation and then the people. There would first be a physical beginning of life and then a resurrection of relationship.

CHAPTER 46

The Final Embrace: The Empty Cup

The final piece would be the resurrection of relationship, the final statement of the bringing together of these two personalities.
I thought that there had to be a visual connection to the beginning. The cup of suffering in Gethsemane, then full, had to now be shown as empty. I battled with this thought: Gethsemane had shown that the crucifixion had been the will of the Father, had then the cup of suffering for the Jewish people also been willed by the Father? Sometimes I ask the questions, but I know that I do not have the possibility of being given the answer, so I sculpt.

I sculpted the two figures, half of their bodies coming out of the stones, stones that represented the dead.
Jesus had given himself to the drinking of the cup, so He had to be the one holding it, raising the empty cup above them both as they embrace each other because they have recognized each other's suffering. For me, this piece, with its life-giving embrace, would be the piece that would bring a future hope.

The word "payback" that had begun this whole process was to be fulfilled during a time of unprecedented grace and favor in which God Himself would restore to the Jewish people all that had been taken from them, all that the enemy had ravaged against them.
This, I believe, is His prayer, and it is now my prayer, that God will remember the six million and pay back all that was taken from His people as a result of the Holocaust. I am always asking myself, Has the "Fountain of Tears" been an expression of this prayer? Does it communicate the 'payback' word somehow? I see this creative journey as an intercession, something that the Lord has begun.

At some point it will have an end, there will be a completion.

One moment I even asked the Lord, not really being too serious and not really expecting an answer, "When will this intercession end?" Suddenly I was shocked, and I felt an immediate response from the Lord. I felt Him say, "When Jerusalem is a praise in all the earth". It was direct and abrupt; it felt deep and conclusive.

When Jesus is fully King, then Jerusalem would be a praise in all the earth. When would this be? I thought this could be a very long intercession. Or maybe not?
I felt that He had said that there was an end. But the timing was within His hands, and I would leave it with Him.

CHAPTER 47

A "Fountain of Tears" in Arad

The "Fountain" went through its different building stages and now sits fully erected, basically in the closed court of our backyard. We live in Arad, a small, desert city in the Judean wilderness, an area of Israel, about a two and a half hour drive south of Jerusalem. When explaining the "Fountain" to the many different groups who come to see the work, I learn something new each time, but never as much as from the Holocaust survivors who have come. Their responses have surprised us and taken our understanding to a much deeper level.

In general, Israelis are shocked when they first enter the "Fountain's" courtyard because they are immediately confronted with the two personalities of the crucifixion and the Holocaust. While they recognize the visual elements, they don't understand their connection, because these two personalities have been separated for over two thousand years. On the one hand, they are shocked by what they see, but on the other hand, they also feel drawn.

Probably our most dramatic encounter was with a businesswoman who worked with the Arad municipality. Hearing about the "Fountain", it was not clear to her what we were doing, so she decided to make time for a visit. When she called us to arrange the day and time, she underlined the fact that she would have only fifteen minutes between her other appointments.
Upon arrival, Lili took a few steps, stopped and stared at the panels. She put one hand over her mouth and the other on her chest.
     "I can't breathe! I can't breathe!..." she kept repeating and then turned to me with, "You have taken the two hardest things in our history and laid them on the same table! The mayor has to see this!" Immediately, she began to make phone calls and as a result of Lili's visit, we had three different groups from the municipality visit us.

Usually it is the Israelis who ask us, "Why isn't this a public site?" They want everyone to see the "Fountain". Their response has been the opposite reaction to the work from what I had expected.
Oh, yes, people have been angry and even enraged. I feel that any reaction is good; it shows there has been a response to something that may have lain dormant but now was stirred and now cannot be neglected.
Israelis want to hear my story, the process of how the "Fountain" came to be, what compelled me to dare to touch this subject of the Holocaust and, even more so, to compare it with the crucifixion.
It is hard for me to give a conclusive answer, because at the beginning I had no agenda in mind as to what this work would be or say.

The "Fountain of Tears" is my response to what I felt the Lord was putting on me, even a glimpse of what is in His own heart. In the end, only a question remains: why the suffering, the pain and sense of abandonment?

Art has many layers of communication, and each visitor teaches us by telling us what they see. The main thing we discover is that the language of art bypasses the human intellect and touches the heart. People then speak out of the position of their heart that sometimes gives expression to deeper places within them. Their words are a surprise to us and sometimes also to themselves.

Some Israeli's will ask, "Was this commissioned or did you pay for this yourself?" They want to know if we are the real source of the work. When they discover that it was funded by Dafna and me, they then start with a list of questions. They hear our Hebrew explanations and are amazed that we as Gentiles have Israeli citizenship. Can't understand why we wanted it. But then they ask the main question,
"Did you do the army here?"
This always carries a lot of significance when I say, "Yes." Then they continue, "Do you have children?" "Yes, two boys." "Have they also done the army?" "Yes." Without saying more, there is a sense that comes, "You belong to us, you are not so naïve, you fully understand what you have done here. Now talk to me and tell me 'Why?'"

Geoff Barnard

CHAPTER 48

A "Fountain of Tears" in Birkenau
The Journey

In a way, the "Fountain of Tears" in Birkenau all began with the story of the model's face for the figure of the Holocaust.

Each time I had to be in Poland or Europe, I would always try to visit Auschwitz in order to find out more about this mysterious man I had seen on the 15 minute introduction movie but still knew so little about.

In 2008, the Lord strongly spoke to me that the year 2012 was going to be a year like I'd never known before. I'm usually cautious about people putting a lot of emphasis on a certain year or predicting events that will happen on specific dates. Most of the time I don't pay attention because this is so often abused with regard to Israel. Many times people have predicted or even prophesied, saying, "This is going to happen then and there," or "in that certain year there is going to be a big war," etc. People are always throwing out dates, and usually nothing happens. Even though I realized that this word of "2012" might be from the Lord, I figured, this being 2008, it was four years away and by that time I would have forgotten all about it. So I put the idea aside.

It was in 2010 that I was together with Geoff, my close friend, for his first visit to Birkenau. I showed him around the camp and its surroundings. The weather was freezing cold with lots of rain - the perfect circumstances for seeing Birkenau, for in this kind of weather one connects better to the memory of the camp. While showing Geoff around, suddenly, out of the blue, as if something got interjected into the whole atmosphere of being in Birkenau, I felt like the Lord saying to me, *The 'Fountain' will be coming here, to Birkenau!* Obviously shocked, I did pay attention.

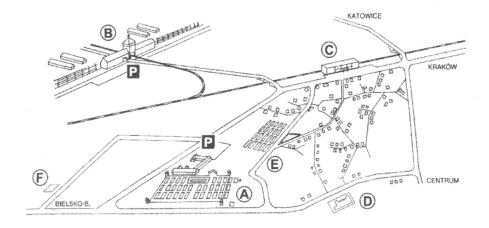

A.   Main camp Auschwitz   B. Birkenau camp

Selection point inside Birkenau - then and now

Through the years I have learned to respond to a "suddenly".
O.k., I thought, *if this is really from the Lord, He will have to confirm it. But I'm not going to seek it out or make it happen.*

During the next six months little things began happening, as if the Lord˙ wanted to remind me about what He had said about Birkenau.
One day, while visiting friends in Krakow, I met a Polish real estate agent. "What would it take to buy a piece of property in Poland?" I asked her without being too specific.

"Where exactly are you thinking?" she asked.

"Well... Brzezinka." I used the Polish name of the village where the Birkenau camp is situated.

Looking surprised, she said, "I'll investigate and if I find something I'll send you an email."

Over the next year, I received several emails with information about property, and each time I was in Poland I would meet with the lady real estate agent over coffee. Besides the real estate agent, Dafna and a few close friends, nobody else knew about the idea. During those 1 ½ - 2 years, thoughts about the "Fountain" in Birkenau kept whirling around in my head.

In July, 2012, I received another email with information about pieces of property that were for sale in Birkenau. As a way of confirmation, one of the things I had asked the Lord was that the piece of property had to have visual contact with the Birkenau concentration camp.
I had already seen several pieces of property, even in the village itself, but the only visual contact those properties had was a corner of the guard post of the camp. I felt it was important to have it right, but at the same time it was rather scary.

"Lord, you really have to 'knock' me down if this is from You," I said. "I have to know, to be sure this is from You. We would be investing so much in this."

In 1941, the so-called Judenrampe in Auschwitz became the selection point for the Jews arriving by cattle cars from all over Europe.

A narrow dirt road, leading off this platform, led to the gates of Birkenau. Those selected for an immediate death in the gas chambers had to walk that road to the distant gates. Those selected to live a little longer walked in the opposite direction - to Auschwitz I, the mother camp. In 1944, Rudolf Hess, the Auschwitz camp commandant, ordered railroad tracks to be laid from the selection point straight into the Birkenau gates. This way, they could process the largest transport of Hungarian Jews to their deaths as quickly as possible.

Those tracks always had an emotional effect on me. My Kibbutz grandmother had been 12 years old when she entered the gates of Birkenau in one of the cattle cars. Upon arrival she immediately was separated from her mother and younger sister, never to see them again. She and her older sister, who was 14, were scheduled to be gassed two weeks later. Somehow they ended up being sent to Germany, and their lives were spared because of their small hands. The Nazi production line needed children's hands to adjust an instrument inside the bombs they produced. By the end of the war both sisters were liberated from Bergen-Belsen.

Due to my special relationship with this kibbutz family, I was emotionally connected to those railroad tracks.

"If this land we're buying has anything to do with the dirt road to the camp or those railroad tracks, that would be the final confirmation I would need," I told the Lord.

In July, 2012, I received an email from the real estate agent who wrote that she might have a piece of property that would interest me. Included were some pictures and a satellite map. The person who took the pictures stood in front of the property, showing all directions. Because I had been in that area so often, I thought I might recognize something and know exactly where it was taken.

In the corner of one of the pictures, I noticed part of something that looked like a gate. Surprised, I enlarged it and then recognized the gates into the Birkenau camp. Immediately I knew exactly where this piece of property was! The plot was attached to the dirt road; in order to reach the property you had to cross the railroad tracks which Hess had created.

Shocked, I realized that this was the property, and now I had to respond. Dafna and I decided that the only thing to do was to make an offer to the real estate agent.

"How much are they asking for the property?" I asked her.

"95.000 Zlotys," she said.

That would be $30.000. Dafna and I figured we could pay $5,000. *What are the Polish procedures for buying property?* I wondered. *Do we make an offer? Do you dicker? What is the usual protocol?*

We decided to tackle the problem like an Israeli. "They asked Zl. 95,000, so we'll offer them Zl. 65,000," I suggested to Dafna.

I gave the real estate agent our price, and we went off to visit different friends. All the time I kept texting the real estate agent, asking about their response to our offer and expecting them to begin negotiating. We didn't hear from them for one-and-a-half long weeks.

"Perhaps I've insulted them," I told Dafna. "Perhaps the offer was so low they won't even bother to reply. Perhaps I I've wrecked our chance."

Dafna had to return home to Israel, but I stayed behind for another three days to meet some friends from Holland and England who knew about the property and wanted to see it. While showing them the piece of property, I received a text message from the real estate agent. "They've accepted your offer!" That was all it said. No dickering about the price, nothing. However, at the bottom of the text she wrote, "But there is one condition."

I immediately phoned her. "What is the condition?"

"They're willing to accept the offer," she told me, "but you have to close the deal quickly."

In Israel, fast closure means within 24 hours. "What is fast in Poland?" I asked her.

After checking with the owners, the lady called me back, "You have to close the deal within two months."

For me, this was a huge amount of time to come up with the sum of Zl. 65,000, equivalent to $20,000.

We would pay $5,000 of our own money towards this amount and knew we had to keep quiet and not ask people for money.

Only a core group of people knew about the project.

Back in Arad, our friend Geoff, who knew a little bit about what was going on in Poland, came over to our house.

"I know something is happening in Poland and I also know it has something to do with property," he said. "I'm not sure what's happening, but if you and Dafna are thinking about buying a piece of property, whatever amount of money you're putting into it, Caryl and I are going to match it!"

Surely that was a gutsy thing to say! So when I told Geoff about the property, they too put $5,000 towards the sum we needed to buy the plot of land.

Two days later, I received a phone call from Cor, the Dutch friend I had met in Poland.

"I know there's something going on with the property," he began. "I'm the head of this Holocaust foundation board in Holland and talked with the other board members. We have decided to support the project with $10,000!"

In exactly three days, the money we needed to buy the property had come in. But then we learned that it was impossible for us, being Israelis and non-EU residents, to buy the property.

About three years earlier, a Dutch group had come to visit the "Fountain of Tears". Cor Roos, a tax consultant, had been so moved by what he saw that he said, "In the Netherlands I represent a foundation for Holocaust memorials. I'm so impressed with your work that I would like to donate $ 8,000, which you can use for PR. Are you an amuta? [Non-profit organization]."

Being a self-employed artist, we had no status as a non-profit organization. We now learned his offer created a technical problem.

"A foundation can only donate money to another foundation, not to an individual. Can't you establish an amuta in Israel?" Cor suggested.

We asked around, checked with friends who had amutot.

In the end Dafna concluded it was too complicated and too expensive, let alone having to deal with the Israeli bureaucracy. When I shared this with Cor, he suggested we register a foundation in Holland, which was a quick and easy process.

Thus, the Fountain of Tears Foundation was created, and as the principal artist, I could draw money from this fund. The amuta had been created to channel that particular gift of $ 8,000. It had been the first and last donation that had come in.

Perhaps we can buy the land through this foundation, I thought.
"Is the FOT Foundation still active?" I asked Cor.
"Yes, I've kept it alive, even though it's asleep at the moment," Cor said. "It's just a matter of waking it up again."
Eventually, the Fountain of Tears Foundation was able to buy the Birkenau property within the two months' time frame. From the first donations we were able to buy the land, hire an architect and create the designs.

And then I remembered the word the Lord had given me four years previously, **"Pay attention to the year 2012! It will be a year like you've never known before!"**
Looking back over that year, I realized more amazing things had happened. Throughout the year 2011, I had been busy with all kinds of projects in different places. And then suddenly, at the end of that year, everything seemed to have dried up. There were possibilities of work, but nothing materialized. Until August, 2012, I had not sold one piece of art and neither had I been working on a commission. As we had earned enough in the 1½ years before, there was sufficient money to get us through 2012. There seemed always to be something going on in Poland and Germany. Because I didn't have any commissions to work on, I was able to participate in those events almost every month.

It was amazing to see how God provided the finances for the Birkenau project. Even though I didn't have income for almost an entire year, I was able to fly to Poland whenever I was needed to make preparations for the project.

By 2013, we had worked on the architectural drawings. Again, because there was no other work or commission demanding my time or attention, I could focus on Birkenau.

Drawings and plans for the Fountain in Birkenau

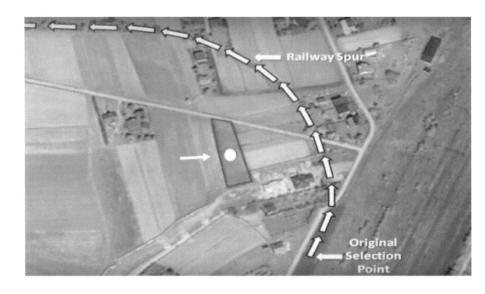

That was fine for a certain period of time, but finally I complained to the Lord. "Enough, Lord! A commission would be good now!" Nothing happened. There were possibilities and proposals and certain commissions would certainly have happened in the past, but this time – nothing. At one point I got a little desperate with the Lord, "It has been a long time, Lord!"

But my heavenly Father knew that I would not be able to focus on Birkenau the way I was doing now if there was something else demanding my attention. I had to be totally focused on this project. But still, I tried, "It would be good to have a little income, Lord!"

Even my accountant for over 16 years began to wonder. "You're doing a lot of flying! You're supposed to be working on something in Poland, but there is no income. You're spending a lot of money, but is there something coming in?" My accountant told me, "I know you have your ups and downs, but the trouble is that you're spending lots of money and you're doing castings and all this, but if you don't have income, this looks really bad."

Trying to explain to him in a way he would understand, I said, "Listen, I'm working on a large project in Poland right now and it is going to take two, maybe three, years in which money is only going out." I hoped that he would understand that, like in any business endeavor, one invests in the hope that money will come in eventually.

"I can carry this with the income tax authorities for three years," he replied, "but then you're going to have to show me some kind of income."

"Ok," I said, thinking, I've got a year's breathing space for now. My accountant understands me to a certain degree. He knows I'm a believer and that I'm doing all these projects.

We have become good friends and there are moments that he feels secure enough to ask me personal questions.

Suddenly, I received a commission with the Bible Society in Jerusalem and even sold a few smaller pieces here and there.

Is this from the Lord? I wondered, so I asked, "Are You sure You really want me to take on the Bible Society's request? Should I do this?" I had almost become used to not having large commissions anymore.

Being so focused on the Birkenau project now, I didn't want to lose that special communion with the Lord if I accepted the commission. However, the Lord allowed me to accept it, which meant that for 2014 there was some income. My accountant was going to be very happy, so perhaps the Lord did this for him.

The financial aspect of the whole project is such that we always have enough for the work at hand. From the first donations we were able to buy the land, build the workshop and put in a driveway. The Lord always graciously provides when we are ready to take the next step. It's a faith project, not a for-profit one. After many considerations, I decided to build the wall and make the panels in Birkenau instead of shipping them from Israel to Poland.
In the end, we calculated it would be more cost-effective to build a foundry on the premises and do the casting at the location itself.

The Israeli airport security always wants to know what I'm carrying in those big boxes.
"These are portions of a piece of artwork that I'm doing in Poland," I explain. "I'm a sculptor. This is the wax, the stage before casting."
The weird-looking packages only show portions of the sculpture. Usually they don't understand what I'm saying, but are nevertheless fascinated because they've never met a sculptor before.
Then the security staff takes me aside and begins to ask all kinds of personal questions like, "What's it like to be a sculptor? You do all the work yourself?"
They are always very generous by allowing me to carry those strange items on the plane.

I felt a holy fear in entering into this geographical space of Birkenau. If there was a reflection in the "Fountain" of the relationship between the Holocaust and the crucifixion, Birkenau, in my mind, represented Golgotha for the Jewish people just as Jerusalem had been the Golgotha for the crucifixion.

Birkenau represented a geographical space unlike any other on the planet. There had been more Jewish blood shed there than any other place on the earth. The ground for kilometers around the camp would have been saturated with ash, the ash of Jewish corpses coming out of those chimneys. The crematoriums had burned 24 hours a day, 7 days a week. I felt that there had to be a prayer house created in relationship to the "Fountain" that would be active night and day in the same way that the ovens had burned night and day. I even had a sense that the land around the camp belonged to Israel; it had, in a way, been bought by blood, Jewish blood.

I had many thoughts and feeling in these beginning steps. I had hoped sometimes that the Lord would pause the momentum, even say to me, "Well done. You don't have to go any further. You get credit with me for your willingness."

But the word that kept coming was "**no delays!**"

We began to see this over and over again.

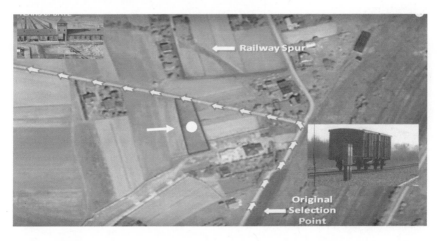

The plans for the building went through and were accepted in the end of July of 2014. The first step would be foundations. We started to investigate cement contractors. This always takes a long time and as the summer was ending no one wanted to pour cement close to the beginning of winter. Then a contractor came along with a good bid and was willing to start in the beginning of October.

It took two weeks to prepare and pour the cement for the foundation of the building.

The ready concrete foundations. The small building serves as Rick's workshop and mini-foundry to enable the reconstruction of the full size bronze figures of the Holocaust survivor for the Fountain of Tears.

The first two weeks of October in Poland can already be serious winter, but that year they had what they call a Polish golden fall, weather that they hadn't had for 14 years. The weather was beautiful for the two weeks of the preparing and pouring of the cement. We made it in time before winter, and now I thought we could rest till the spring. No one would work over the winter.

Back in Israel in mid-November, I received a call from a good friend from Vermont, USA. He is an expert in wood construction. (This is the construction system that we had decided to use in building the building for the "Fountain".) I hadn't talked to him in a long time and was surprised by the phone call. He started out by saying that he and his partner had some spare time and thought that they might want to help with the building if I needed it. I got excited, thinking that these guys were the best of the best at this kind of construction. I presumed that they wanted to invest a few days on their way to visit Israel. Perhaps they could help get things started in Poland. They even might want to come in the spring, when it would be warm enough to work.

"That would be great," I told them. "When do you think about coming? And how much time would you have?"

"We can come in a week and a half and can stay there for five weeks," my friend responded.

Shocked, I said, "But what about the weather?"

"We work in Vermont, also in the middle of the winter," he told me. "We know how to deal with the winter weather."

Everything happened so fast! A week and a half later I was back in Poland to collect them at the airport.

A Polish friend had arranged an apartment for them for the entire time and it was fantastic. The weather was cold and snowy, but ever morning I would pick them and we would work each day.

There were no delays in wood supplies, no delays in tools, no delays in money, no delays at all. All the walls were constructed.

It was amazing to watch this happen knowing that the Lord was so behind it all. Shortly after my arrival back in Israel in January, a close German friend called me about the "Saxony Friends of Israel". This group of German craftsmen were interested in helping with the building of the "Fountain" in Auschwitz. Again, I was surprised at the timing of this call.

When I told him how much was now completed on the building he said, "Great! We can do the roof."
The roof was complicated because of the width of the exhibition area that would house the "Fountain". I told him that I was waiting for the engineer's plans on the steel support construction that would have to go in first before they could build the big roof. His reply was, "Hurry up with that. We are planning to come in the beginning of March."

I had to go back to Poland and meet with a steel company and make some decisions, sign a contract and head home. Now came the prayer that the Polish steel workers would get their work done and in place before the Germans arrived. There also had to be a huge delivery of wood that the Germans would need after the Poles finished doing the steel. Everything had to work within a very tight time frame, but I kept pushing. The Germans would be arriving ready to tear into the work on the 9th of March; the Polish steel workers were promising to try and be done by this date.

Another complication was that Dafna and I had already booked tickets to be in Canada from the 1st of March till the 20th for my 60th birthday and to see my Dad and our sons. So this would mean that I would have to manage all of this online.
The Germans arrived on time on the 9th; the Poles were delayed by one day till the 10th. But on the day that they couldn't work, the German workmen were given time to visit the camps of Auschwitz and Birkenau, which was more important. Within three very full days of work, the great roof was built and covered with a waterproof seal. There had been a lot of skype calls and emails and money transfers, but it all came off, without a delay. How totally amazing the Lord's grace is!

Dafna and I are aware of certain elements of time: The plot of land for the "Fountain" was bought in 2012. This year was a 70 year marker in the history of Birkenau. Seventy years before, in 1942, a decision was made by the upper level SS in the German army concerning all the Jews of Europe. They called it the "final solution to the Jewish problem".

On January 23, 1942, the decision was made that all the Jews of Europe would be killed by gassing and burning the bodies. In the spring of 1942, Birkenau was birthed and it would become the largest killing center within the Nazi regime.

Also in 2012, for the first time in Israel's history as a nation, the Jewish population of the country came to 6 million. The Lord had promised in the "payback" word that He was going to redeem the number 6 million, so that what had always been a number that represented death to the Jewish people would be turned into a number that represented life.

It had always amazed me that the Jewish people had not only survived the Holocaust but had formed a country three years after its end. There have been threats of annihilation over this nation from its birth until now. Yet they now stand at the marker of 70 years after a decision that was made that took 6 million of their people. They stand with that number restored or paid back to them, not just to them as an ethnic group that survived genocide, but as a Jewish nation back within their own land.

2012, as a 70 year marker, was also a beginning marker for the next three years. There would be a series of these markers up until January of 2015 which would then be the 70 year memorial to the liberation of Auschwitz.

Chapter 49

The Return of the "Lion of Judah"

The return of the "Lion of Judah" is also very much connected to the building in Birkenau.

Even though so much happened to me at the 'Payback' conference, there was something else that occurred at the same time. Back then it seemed small in comparison. After the final meeting of the conference people stood around talking before leaving. Graham, who was surrounded by people, called me over to introduce me to his close friends from California - Tim and Darlene. After introductions, Tim, in a very direct way, said he was interested in a sculpture of a lion. "Darlene and I are buying a new home which has a large wall in the living room," he explained. He envisioned a lion on the wall.
Even though I was surprised by Tim's decisiveness, I only listened halfheartedly, as I kept thinking on the 'payback' word. I still didn't understand what it could mean. Often, at the end of conferences people are wound up with emotions and say things that they don't necessarily mean so I tried to be polite and engaging. "Is the wall fully square? And roughly, what are the measurements?" I asked him.
Tim pointed his finger to a panel on the ceiling of the church and said that the wall was about the same dimensions as that panel.
The panel was quite big so I thought, *He wants a fairly big lion and the panel is rectangular, going more vertical than horizontal, so the lion probably will be standing.*
He answered my additional questions, but still I didn't take his request too seriously. Tim scribbled his phone number in the USA on a piece of scrap paper, and I thanked him and said goodbye to everyone.

The months that followed were consumed with the struggle connected to what the Lord showed us in relationship to the 'payback' word.

The idea of a lion on a wall in California barely crossed my mind. But then, while we were in North Carolina that summer, along with many 'suddenlies' that were happening to us in relation to the "Fountain", I suddenly remembered Tim and Darlene. After finding the piece of paper on which Tim had written his number, I wondered what to do. Months had passed since that first conversation, but in the end I decided I would phone them. *Maybe they are not at home,* I thought. *Then at least I have made an attempt to contact them.*
Darlene answered the phone after the second ring and immediately remembered who I was.

"How is it going with the Lion?" she wanted to know.

Trying not to lie, I said, "I think the 'Lion' is fine".

"Can we see the drawings?" She told me they would send me a ticket to California in a few weeks and that the beginning of September would be good for them.
I got off the phone, a little shocked, thinking, *I better take this seriously!*

There are many kinds of lions and I didn't have any idea how I would start this drawing. Trying to remember the conversation between Tim and myself, I recalled that he said he loved the lions at Trafalgar Square in London. However, those lions are lying down and, if I remembered correctly, the wall in his home was more vertical. This meant the lion would have to be standing.

ABRAHAM MELNIKOV Monument to the Defenders of Tel-Chai. 1926. Stone. Kibbutz Kfar Giladi

I decided the local library would have some books on lions and maybe this would help me start the process. Wandering around the library my eye fell on the section "Israel" and I picked out a book with pictures of Israel. On the back page there was a large picture of the Trumpeldor lions at Tel Hai.

I had never been there but knew a little history about Trumpeldor. One of his famous quotes was, "Good to die for our country". There were two stone lions that marked a memorial site for him. The stance of the lions really struck me - they were roaring upward and sitting very vertical. I could feel something beginning to happen. I checked the book out and started to do some drawings, using the pictures of these lions as references.

Over the next few days I did many sketches. They became much more detailed than the pictures and went beyond those of Trumpeldor's lions. I found myself drawing a crucifixion scene interwoven into the lion's mane. By using the lines of the hair you could and could not see it. Then to the right of the crucifixion scene, I started to sketch what could be perceived as a religious Jew holding Torah scrolls. Then I did another man and then another, almost like one layer after another until the figure disappeared completely into the hair of the lion.

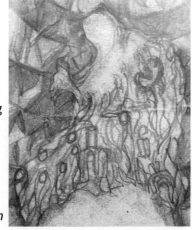

This is like the dispersions of the Jewish people from different countries, *throughout history,* I thought. The last person to leave would be the rabbi carrying the Torah scrolls. It was as if these overlaying figures were moving down the right side of the mane of the lion. At the bottom of the mane, close to where the body begins but still in the mane, was a menorah, upside down and floating in the hair. For me, this menorah represented the Diaspora. Like the Jewish people them-selves, out of the Land of Israel and not in a right position, so the menorah is upside down and floating. I now went to the left of the crucifixion scene and started to draw crematorium doors from the Holocaust. There was an open door with a chimney rising upward from the door. The entire drawing was incorporated into the hair of the mane.

There was smoke coming out of the chimney forming six surreal figures moving downward into the part of the mane covering the chest of the lion. I felt that one of the figures would be proportionately much smaller than the others. This would represent the million and a half Jewish children killed in the Holocaust. All of these smaller drawings were interwoven into the hair of the lion, seen and not seen. The lion I drew was sitting on twelve large stones that I knew would represent the twelve tribes of Israel. This image just seemed to pour out of me; I didn't understand, but I knew I had been caught in something special. When the drawing was finished I knew this would be the "Lion of Judah".

I didn't know what Tim and Darlene's expectations were, but it didn't seem to matter right then. They sent me a ticket and I flew to California. Darlene picked me up at the airport and we got to know each other as we chatted on the drive back to their old house. They would be moving into the new house with this mysterious wall in a few weeks. I would stay a few days with them and then head back to North Carolina.

Tim arrived home after work, and we greeted each other. He immediately wanted to see the drawing. I was a little nervous, wondering what their reaction would be to the "Lion".
While they went over the drawing, now spread out on the dining room table, I sat in a chair off to the side. There seemed to be some tension and whispered words until Tim came over to me.
    "This drawing isn't even close to what I expected," he said and went back to the table. A few moments later he returned. "You don't know what you have drawn here. This is not at all what I would have wanted in a lion, but this is exactly what it should be. I just found out a few weeks ago that I have Jewish heritage in my family that has been hidden for generations."
I surmised that this decision to hide the Jewishness in Tim's family was because of the Holocaust. Many Jews that survived the Holocaust knew that they were persecuted because they were Jews, and so they decided that they would bury that part of their life and no longer be Jews.

211

 In the end the "Lion of Judah" was produced in bronze, sitting on the 12 stones, three meters high by three a half meters across the bottom, completely dominating the living room of Tim and Darlene's new home.

The "Lion of Judah" became a marker, the first piece in which I had combined the crucifixion and Holocaust.

Many years later, as January 27, 2015, came closer, Dafna and I were asked to be a part of a prayer conference in Auschwitz, marking 70 years since the liberation of the camp. We had agreed to be there, but at the same time I had been working on a full-sized lion which I hoped would be ready before that date. Called  the "Vengeance of the Lamb", it is similar to the "Lion of Judah". It also sits on twelve stones and roars upward, but in this sculpture there is a small lamb between the lion's front paws. The lamb is dead, sacrificed, and the lion, through his roar, proclaims his attachment to this lamb and his declaration of revenge. In his mane is not the Holocaust, as in the first lion sculpture, but a large menorah, fully upright, interwoven in the hair. Because the Jewish people are back in the Land the menorah is standing properly.

Even though I had hoped that the vengeance of the Lamb lion could be done before the 27th, I realized that this was impossible.

About a week before we were leaving for Poland, I was in Jerusalem trying to get a few things done and feeling a little pressured time-wise. On the way home, I felt more relaxed. We could start getting our bags packed to go to Auschwitz. While driving, I was pondering a few things when all of a sudden I felt the Lord very strongly say to me that I had to take the lion and also that I had to write out in Hebrew, "Oh, Lord, that my head would be a spring of water and my eyes a fountain of tears that I would weep day and night for the slain of my people".

Furthermore, on the 27th of January, I was to put the Israeli flag on the building. The presence of the Lord was so strong and He said so much that I had to pull the car off the road and write everything down. "But the lion isn't done yet," I told the Lord.

You do have a lion! The Lord told me. Suddenly I remembered. *Yes, I still have the mold from the original lion, but I will have to find it and clean it. And how will I do the Hebrew letters for these verses from Jeremiah?*

At that time the building in Birkenau was only partially constructed and the outside covered with chip board. *Should I cut out templates for the words and paint them on the wall?* I felt that these temporary displays would be a marker for this particular date. If I could find the mold of the lion after all these years and make a simple cast of the pieces in plaster - that might work. But the flag, that scared me a bit. Putting an Israeli flag on the building in this little Polish village (Brezinka) Birkenau, could result in some very negative responses from the neighbors. But as this really seemed to be from the Lord, I knew I had to try.

Dafna was a huge help by creating the templates for the letters. I found the pieces of the mold, cleaned them and cast the white plaster. *I may be able to find the Israeli flag at the prayer conference*, I thought. We worked hard right up until the day we flew. I managed to cast the pieces for the "Lion" and wrapped them with rope and tape in what I hoped I could use as a carry-on bag for the flight. It was way oversized and weighed close to 40 kilograms and looked very strange.

At the airport it was as if no one saw the carry-on lion. I had to carry the bag about 20 meters and then rest and switch hands until we finally arrived at our gate. Through all the checks, until we were finally sitting down in our seats on the plane, no one said a word of protest about my lion.

Upon arrival in Oswiecim (Auschwitz), we settled into our room. Because we had a few days before the 27th, I immediately began constructing the pieces of the "Lion of Judah" on the outside wall of our building in Birkenau. Using twelve large, flat stones I created the base for the lion to sit on.

עמי|בת|חללי|את|וליל ה|יומם|אבכה

We painted the Hebrew words on a smooth piece of wood and mounted them beside the lion. I had found an Israeli flag, and mounted it on the front of the building on the morning of the 27th. That day, delegates of all the nations commemorated the 70 year marker of the liberation of Auschwitz at the entrance to the Birkenau camp.

A few hundred meters away from this large international meeting stood a half-built edifice that was marked by the cry of Jeremiah the prophet, by the Lion of Judah roaring His intercession over the suffering of the Jewish people, and by the Israeli flag proclaiming the existence of the nation that God had birthed out of such a death.

The "Lion", the beginning within this journey, has marked each step. I pray that His roar over the Jewish people and over the land of Israel will bring full restoration and will bring all Israel back to Himself.

In 2015, construction began in full for the building that will eventually house the "Fountain" and the message of the "Fountain". Will it be finished this year? Only the Lord knows.

But I am convinced that the Lion has begun to roar and that there will be no delays.

APPENDIX

From bare wall to "Fountain of Tears"

Humble beginnings - at first there was no roof over the exhibition.

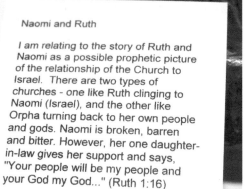

Naomi and Ruth

I am relating to the story of Ruth and Naomi as a possible prophetic picture of the relationship of the Church to Israel. There are two types of churches - one like Ruth clinging to Naomi (Israel), and the other like Orpha turning back to her own people and gods. Naomi is broken, barren and bitter. However, her one daughter-in-law gives her support and says, "Your people will be my people and your God my God..." (Ruth 1:16)

One of the seven olive trees outside the building that receive the
water from the 'Tears' flowing over the stone dividers inside the building.

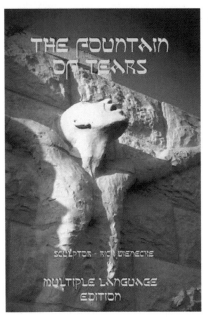

The curriculum is designed to be covered in a series of 1½-2 hour meetings, ideally one section per week.

The Fountain of Tears DVD has multiple language tracks: English; Hebrew; French; German; Dutch; Spanish; Polish; Russian; Greek; Cantonese; Korean; Portuguese

A Dialogue of Suffering Between the Crucifixion and the Holocaust is a curriculum designed to be used for personal use or small study groups. This book also contains many pictures of the Fountain of Tears. Not meant to be an intellectual exercise, this study tool delves deeper in the connection and similarities that exist between the Crucifixion and the Holocaust.
The material is based on the 'The Fountain of Tears', a sculptured dialogue of suffering between the Crucifixion and the Holocaust. Don't expect to find clear-cut answers, but allow God the Father to share His tears one layer at a time, in the questions.

ISBN 978-965-7542-29-3

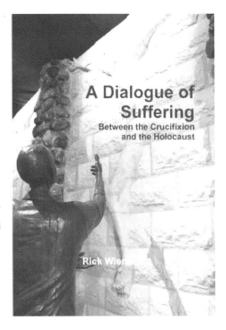

Fountain of Tears

Website: http://www.castingseeds.com
Email: castingseeds@gmail.com

Visits to the Fountain of Tears MUST be pre-arranged. The Sculpture is situated on private property and is not a public site. Appointments need to be made in advance. A visit to the Fountain will last between 60 and 90 minutes. Generally, the presentation is in English but several other languages can be accommodated. There is no admission fee.

To arrange a visit, email us with details of possible dates and times. Please state the anticipated number in the group and the preferred language.

Fountain of Tears Foundation

Website; http://fot-foundation.org

The foundation is registered in the Chamber of Commerce for East Netherlands, number 50086286.

Donations for the Fountain of Tears project in Birkenau can be made through the Foundation and are tax deductible